AN
ENGLISHMAN,
AN
IRISHMAN
AND A
SCOTSMAN ...

First published in Great Britain in 2010 by
Michael O'Mara Books Limited
9 Lion Yard
Tremadoc Road
London SW4 7NQ

Copyright © Michael O'Mara Books Limited 2010

A CIP catalogue record for this book is available from the British Library.

Papers used by Michael O'Mara Books Limited are natural, recyclable products
made from wood grown in sustainable forests. The manufacturing processes
conform to the environmental regulations of the country of origin.

ISBN: 978-1-84317-500-1

1 2 3 4 5 6 7 8 9 10

www.mombooks.com

Title page illustration by Andrew Pinder

Designed and typeset by Design 23

Printed and bound in Great Britain by CPI Cox & Wyman, Reading, RG1 8EX

AN ENGLISHMAN, AN IRISHMAN AND A SCOTSMAN ...

NICK HARRIS

MICHAEL O'MARA BOOKS LIMITED

Contents

Introduction

An Englishman, an Irishman and a Scotsman walked into a bar. The barman said: 'Is this some kind of joke?'

The answer is, probably, 'Yes'. We've been telling jokes about Englishmen, Irishmen and Scotsmen for years (for some reason the Welsh have never been considered funny enough and, anyway, where jokes are concerned, four's a crowd). These gags play on national stereotypes in a largely affectionate manner, although in these politically correct times such jokes may be considered offensive by some in the same way that repeatedly asking the chicken why it crossed the road may be deemed a violation of the bird's privacy and an infringement of its human rights.

But don't let the title of this book fool you. There are jokes here on a whole range of subjects – the battle of the sexes, cannibals, children, doctors, drunks, music, religion, sport and working life, to name but a few. If you can't find a good laugh here then I'm a Dutchman. Which reminds me: Did you hear the one about the Dutchman, the German and the Belgian …?

Animals

Deep within a forest a little turtle began to climb a tree. After hours of effort he reached the top, jumped into the air waving his front legs and crashed to the ground. After recovering, he slowly climbed the tree again, jumped and fell to the ground. The turtle tried again and again while a couple of birds sitting on a branch watched his sad efforts. Finally, the female bird turned to her mate. 'Dear,' she chirped, 'I think it's time to tell him he's adopted.'

Four men were playing the last hole of their local golf course. When the final golfer drove off the tee, he hooked into a cow pasture. He advised his friends to play through and said he would meet them at the clubhouse. They followed the plan and waited for their friend.

Half an hour later he appeared, dishevelled, bloody and badly beaten up. They all wanted to know what had happened.

He explained: 'I went over to the cow pasture but could not find my ball. However, I noticed a cow wringing her tail in obvious pain. So I went over and lifted her tail and saw a golf ball solidly embedded. It was a yellow ball so I knew it wasn't mine. Then this woman came out of the bushes. She seemed to be searching for her lost golf ball so I lifted the cow's tail and asked: "Does this look like yours?" That's the last thing I can remember.'

How do you get five donkeys on a fire engine?
—Two in the front, two in the back and one on the roof going 'Ee-Aw-Ee-Aw ...'

Two men went bear hunting. While one stayed in the cabin, the other went out looking for a bear. He soon found a huge bear, shot at it but only wounded it. As the enraged bear charged towards him, the hunter dropped his rifle and started running for the cabin as fast as he could.

He ran pretty fast but the bear was just a little faster and gained on him with every step. Just as the hunter reached the open cabin door, he tripped and fell flat on his face. Too close behind to stop, the bear tripped over him and went rolling into the cabin.

The hunter jumped up, closed the cabin door and yelled to his friend inside: 'You skin this one while I go and get another one!'

A man walked into a bar with a giraffe. He went up to the bar and took a seat, and the giraffe did the same. The man ordered a beer for himself and a double Scotch for the giraffe.

They both downed their drinks and after a while they ordered the same again. They continued drinking for the rest of the evening until suddenly the giraffe fell off his stool and lay unconscious on the floor.

Without saying a word, the man got up and headed

for the door. The barman shouted at him: 'You can't leave that lyin' 'ere!'

The man replied: 'It's not a lion, it's a giraffe.'

Mr Bear and Mr Rabbit were walking through the woods one day when they came across a golden frog. The frog turned to them and said: 'I don't often meet anyone in these parts, but when I do I always give them six wishes. You can have three wishes each.'

Mr Bear immediately wished that all the other bears in the forest were females. The frog granted his wish.

After thinking for a while, Mr Rabbit, who was not overly fond of Mr Bear, said that he wished for a crash helmet. One appeared immediately and he placed it on his head.

Mr Bear was amazed at Mr Rabbit's wish but carried on with his second wish. He wished that all the bears in the neighbouring forests were females as well and the frog granted his wish.

Mr Rabbit then wished for a motorcycle. It appeared before him and he climbed on board and started revving the engine.

Mr Bear could not believe it and complained that Mr Rabbit had wasted two wishes that he could have had for himself. Shaking his head, Mr Bear made his final wish – namely, that all the female bears found him utterly irresistible, making him the most desirable bear in the area.

The frog replied that it had been done and they both turned to Mr Rabbit for his last wish. Mr Rabbit revved the engine, thought for a second, then said: 'I wish that Mr Bear was gay,' and rode off as fast as he could.

Three dogs were sitting in the waiting room of a vet's surgery. The first dog asked the second dog: 'What are you here for?'

'I poop all over the house,' said the second dog, 'so I'm going to be put to sleep. What are you here for?'

The first dog replied: 'Whenever my master is out, I tear the house apart. I bite and chew on everything. I'm going to be put to sleep, too.'

The two dogs looked to the third dog and asked: 'What are you here for?'

The third dog answered: 'Well, one day my mistress was bent over, vacuuming the floor and I just couldn't help myself and I humped her.'

'That's really bad!' exclaimed the others. 'No wonder you're being put to sleep!'

The third dog replied: 'Oh, I'm not being put to sleep. I'm just here to get my nails clipped.'

A zebra had lived her entire life in a zoo and because she was getting on a bit, the zoo keeper decided as a treat that she could spend her final years in bliss on a farm. The zebra was really excited about the prospect of moving to a new home and she stepped out of the horse box to see this huge space with green grass, hills, trees and all these strange animals.

Spotting a big, weird-looking, brown creature, she ran up to it. She said: 'Hi! I'm a zebra, what are you?'

'I'm a cow,' the animal replied.

'Right, and what do you do?' asked the zebra.

'I make milk for the farmer,' said the cow.

The zebra then saw this funny looking little white thing and ran over to it. She said: 'Hi, I'm a zebra, what are you?'

'I'm a chicken,' said the bird.

'Oh, right, what do you do?' asked the zebra.

'I make eggs for the farmer,' said the chicken.

Then the zebra saw this very handsome beast that looked almost exactly like her but without the stripes. She ran over to it and said: 'Hi, I'm a zebra, what are you?'

'I am a stallion,' he replied.

'Wow!' said the zebra. 'What do you do?'

The stallion replied: 'Take off your pyjamas, darling, and I'll show you.'

A man walked into a bar with a monkey on his shoulder, ordered a drink and sat down. The monkey sprang off his shoulder, ran down the bar to the olive bowl, swallowed an olive whole, then jumped on to the pool table and swallowed the cue ball whole.

The barman cried out to the man: 'Oh my God, did you see what your monkey just did?'

'What?' asked the man.

The barman said: 'Your monkey just swallowed the cue ball whole.'

'I'm not surprised,' said the man. 'He eats everything in sight. I'll pay for it and we'll leave.'

Two weeks later, the man and his monkey returned. The man ordered his drink and the monkey jumped off his shoulder and ran to the cherry bowl. He grabbed one, shoved it up his butt then pulled it out and swallowed it whole.

Once again the barman cried out: 'Oh my God, did you see what your monkey just did?'

The man said: 'What did he do this time?'

The barman replied: 'He just shoved a cherry up his butt, then swallowed it whole. That was disgusting!'

The man said: 'Well, I'm not surprised, he still eats everything in sight, but ever since that cue ball he checks everything first.'

An Amish lady was trotting down the road in her horse and buggy when she was pulled over by a cop.

'Ma'am, I'm not going to ticket you,' said the officer, 'but I do have to issue you a warning. You have a broken reflector on your buggy.'

'Oh, I'll let my husband Jacob know as soon as I get home,' the woman replied.

The police officer continued: 'That's fine. Another thing, ma'am. I don't like the way that one rein loops across the horse's back and around one of his balls. I consider that to be animal abuse. Have your husband take care of that right away!'

Later that day, the lady is home telling her husband about her encounter with the policeman.

'Well, dear, what exactly did he say?' her husband asked.

'He said the reflector is broken,' the woman answered.

'I can fix that in two minutes. What else?'

'I'm not sure, Jacob,' the woman said. 'Something about the emergency brake.'

A guy with a Doberman Pinscher and a guy with a Chihuahua decided to go to a restaurant and get something to eat.

The guy with the Chihuahua said: 'We can't go in there. We've got dogs with us.'

The guy with the Doberman Pinscher replied: 'Just follow my lead.'

They walked over to the restaurant, the guy with the Doberman Pinscher put on a pair of dark glasses, and started to walk in.

'Sorry, sir. No pets allowed,' announced the doorman.

The guy with the Doberman Pinscher said: 'You don't understand. This is my seeing-eye dog.'

The doorman inquired: 'A Doberman Pinscher?'

'Yes, they're using them now, they're very good.'

The doorman said: 'Very well. Come on in.'

The guy with the Chihuahua also put on a pair of dark glasses and started to walk in. 'Sorry, sir. No pets allowed,' announced the doorman.

The guy with the Chihuahua said: 'You don't understand. This is my seeing-eye dog.'

The doorman inquired: 'A Chihuahua?'

The man threw up his hands in horror and said: 'You mean they gave me a Chihuahua?!'

John went to visit his ninety-year-old grandfather in a very secluded, rural area of Somerset. After spending a great evening chatting the night away, John's grandfather prepared breakfast of bacon, eggs and toast. However, John noticed a film-like substance on his plate and questioned his grandfather.

'Are these plates clean?' John asked.

His grandfather replied: 'They're as clean as cold water can get 'em. Just you go ahead and finish your meal, sonny.'

For lunch the old man made sandwiches. Again, John was concerned about the plates as his appeared to have tiny specks around the edge that looked like dried egg. So he asked: 'Are you sure these plates are clean?'

Without looking up, the old man said: 'I told you before, sonny, those dishes are as clean as cold water can get them. Now don't you fret, I don't want to hear another word about it.'

Later that afternoon, John was setting off for town but as he was leaving, his grandfather's dog started to growl and wouldn't let him pass. John said: 'Grandpa, your dog won't let me get to my car.'

Without diverting his attention from the shelf he was building, the old man shouted: 'Coldwater, go lay down now! You hear me?'

Three mice were sitting in a bar one day talking about how tough they were. The first one drank a shot of whisky, slammed the glass down on the bar and said: 'There isn't a mouse trap in the world that is strong enough to get me. As a matter of fact I like to spring them, catch the bar, do thirty bench presses with it then hop out.'

The second mouse drank a shot of whisky, slammed the glass on the bar and said: 'No rodent poison can kill me. I eat it like candy, and sometimes I grind it up, roll it and smoke it. It's really great stuff.'

The third mouse drank his shot of whisky, slammed it on the bar, got off his stool and started walking towards the door. The first mouse asked him where he was going. The third mouse looked over his shoulder and replied: 'Home to screw the cat.'

A daddy mole, a mummy mole and a baby mole all lived together in a little mole hole. One day, Daddy Mole stuck his head out of the hole, sniffed the air and said: 'Yum! I smell maple syrup!'

Then Mummy Mole stuck her head out of the hole, sniffed the air and said: 'Oh, yum! I smell honey!'

By now Baby Mole was also trying to stick his head out of the hole to sniff the air, but he couldn't because the bigger moles were in the way. This made him whine: 'All I can smell is molasses!'

An elephant was drinking from a watering hole when he saw a turtle out of the corner of his eye. Reacting with immediate swiftness, he ran down to the water's edge, jumped up into the air and landed on the turtle, turning it to a revolting pulp. A giraffe standing nearby noticed this and, faintly sickened, asked the elephant why he'd squashed the turtle.

The elephant calmly replied by saying that particular turtle had given him a nasty bite on his trunk some fifty years earlier, with no provocation, and he had now got his revenge.

'Wow!' said the giraffe. 'You must have an incredible memory.'

'Yes,' nodded the elephant proudly. 'It's turtle recall.'

Army, Navy and Air Force

Several years after retiring from the army, a general chanced upon his former orderly in the street. They chatted for a while and eventually the general persuaded him to come and work for him as a valet.

'It will be just like old times,' the general enthused. 'You'll soon learn the ropes because your duties will be exactly the same as they were in the army. Just do the same as you did back then and you'll be fine.'

The man decided to accept the job offer. So on his first morning at work, at seven o'clock sharp, the ex-orderly entered the ex-general's bedroom, opened the curtains and gently woke the general. He then walked around to the other side of the bed, slapped the general's wife on the bottom and said: 'Okay, sweetheart, it's back to the village for you!'

Drinking at his favourite tavern, a naval commander glanced across and spotted a pirate, complete with a wooden leg, a hook and an eye patch.

Striking up conversation, the commander asked him: 'How did you get the wooden leg?'

'I'll tell thee,' replied the pirate. 'We were at sea when a terrible storm blew up and I was swept overboard into shark-infested waters. A monster shark bit off my leg.'

'That's awful,' said the commander. 'What about the hook? What's the story behind that?'

'I'll tell thee,' said the pirate. 'We attacked an enemy ship and at the height of the battle my right hand was sliced off by an enemy swordsman.'

'How awful for you,' said the commander. 'And the eye patch? How did you come by that?'

'I'll tell thee,' said the pirate. 'One day we were out at sea when a seagull dropping fell into my eye.'

'You lost your eye to a seagull dropping?' said the commander incredulously.

The pirate replied: 'Well, it was my first day with the hook.'

Three war veterans were boasting about the heroic exploits of their ancestors.

One declared proudly: 'At the age of eleven, my great grandfather was a drummer boy at Shiloh.'

The second said: 'My great grandfather went down with Custer at the Battle of Little Big Horn.'

'I'm the only soldier in my family,' confessed the third veteran, 'but I promise you, if my great grandfather were alive today, he'd be the most famous man in the world.'

'Why? What did he do?' asked the others.

'Oh, nothing much. But he'd be 178 years old!'

Two military policemen chased a draftee who was fleeing from an army base. He ran into a convent where he spotted a nun sitting outside.

'Quick, sister,' he pleaded. 'Hide me. I don't want to be drafted and the military police are after me.'

The nun lifted her skirt and told the young man to hide under it.

'You've got nice legs for a nun,' he remarked from beneath the skirt.

'If you look up a little farther,' said the nun, 'you'll find a pair of balls. I don't want to be drafted either!'

What do you get when you drop a piano on an army base?
—A flat major.

An airman, a sailor and a soldier were using the toilet. The airman finished and washed his hands using a lot of soap and water, then dried them with five paper towels. He said: 'In the Air Force we are told to wash and dry thoroughly.'

The sailor finished and washed his hands using very little soap and water before drying them with one paper towel. 'In the Navy,' he explained, 'we are taught to conserve our resources.'

When the soldier finished, he simply walked out, saying: 'In the Army we just don't pee on our hands.'

A cavalryman was galloping down the track in an attempt to catch up with the rest of his regiment when his horse suddenly stumbled and threw him to the ground. Lying on the ground with a broken leg and fearful that enemy troops would appear at any minute, the cavalryman cried out: 'All you saints in heaven, help me get up on my horse!'

With a superhuman effort, he then managed to leap on to the horse's back, only to go straight over the other side. Finding himself on the ground once again, he called to the heavens: 'Okay, just half of you this time!'

While reviewing the troops, the Colonel couldn't help noticing that one soldier had a massive erection. 'Sergeant Major!' shouted the Colonel. 'Give this man thirty days' compassionate home leave.'

Two months later, the Colonel noticed that the same soldier again had an erection. 'Sergeant Major!' he boomed. 'Give this man another thirty days' compassionate home leave!'

Two months later, the same thing happened again, but this time the Colonel's patience had worn thin. 'Sergeant Major!' he barked. 'Has this man not twice been granted compassionate home leave?'

'Yes, he has, sir,' replied the Sergeant Major.

'Then what's his problem?' demanded the Colonel. 'Why has he got a huge erection?'

The Sergeant Major said: 'It's you he's fond of, sir.'

As a crowded airliner prepared to take off, the peace was shattered by a young boy who picked that moment to throw a wild temper tantrum. No matter what his frustrated, embarrassed mother did to try and calm him down, the boy continued to scream furiously and kick the seats around him.

Suddenly, from the rear of the plane, an elderly man in the uniform of an Air Force General could be seen slowly walking forward up the aisle. Stopping the flustered mother with an upraised hand, the white-haired, soft-spoken General leaned down and, motioning towards his chest, whispered something into the boy's ear.

Instantly, the boy calmed down, gently took his mother's hand and quietly fastened his seat belt. All the other passengers burst into spontaneous applause.

As the General slowly made his way back to his seat, one of the cabin attendants touched his sleeve.

'Excuse me, General,' she asked quietly, 'but could I ask you what magic words you used on that little boy?'

The old man smiled serenely and confided: 'I showed him my pilot's wings, service stars and battle ribbons, and explained that they entitle me to throw one passenger out the plane door on any flight I choose.'

In the course of an army training session, a soldier was told to disguise himself as a tree and to remain silent and motionless for the duration of the exercise. He obeyed the order to the letter until suddenly, in the heart of the forest, he leaped into the air and let out a piercing scream.

'What the blazes do you think you're doing?' boomed the Sergeant Major. 'If this had been a real military exercise, your jumping and yelling could have endangered the lives of the entire company.'

'Sorry, sir,' replied the soldier. 'But I can explain. I tried my best to stay quiet and still, even when a flock of pigeons used me for target practice. And I didn't move a muscle when a large dog peed on my lower branches. But when two squirrels ran up the leg of my pants and I heard the bigger squirrel say: "Let's eat one now and save the other one till winter"... it was more than I could take!'

Airman Brown was assigned to the induction centre, where he advised new recruits about their government benefits, especially their GI insurance. The captain gradually became aware that Brown was selling insurance at an unprecedented rate of success – virtually one hundred per cent. Hugely impressed, he decided to stand at the back of the room and listen to Brown's sales pitch.

After explaining the basics of the GI insurance to the new recruits, Brown said: 'If you have GI insurance and go into battle and are killed, the government has to pay $250,000 to your beneficiaries. But if you don't have GI insurance and go into battle and get killed, the government only has to pay out a maximum of $7,500. So who do you think they are going to send into battle first …?'

MILITARY INTELLIGENCE

If the enemy is in range, so are you.

When the pin is pulled, Mr Grenade is not our friend.

Five-second fuses only last three seconds.

If you see a bomb technician running, follow him.

Never tell the Platoon Sergeant you have nothing to do.

If something hasn't broken on your helicopter, it's about to.

Try to look unimportant; they may be low on ammo.

Any ship can be a minesweeper ... once.

Don't draw fire; it irritates the people around you.

The only time your airplane has too much fuel is when it's on fire.

If your attack is going too well, you're walking into an ambush.

When one engine fails on a twin-engine airplane you always have enough power left to get you to the scene of the crash.

Surrounded for months by enemy troops in the jungle, a platoon of soldiers endured a torrid time. All supply routes were cut off and their living conditions became more appalling by the day. Finally, in a bid to lift morale, the Sergeant announced: 'I've got some good news, men. We're going to have a change of underwear.'

The men breathed a small sigh of relief.

The Sergeant continued: 'Right. Matthews, you change with Finch. Finch, you change with Stefanowski ...'

The Admiral was relaxing in his quarters when the lookout burst in and announced: 'Two enemy ships spotted on the horizon, sir.'

'Very well,' said the Admiral firmly. 'Fetch me my red shirt.'

The immediate danger of attack passed but later that day the lookout burst in again. 'Four enemy ships spotted on the horizon, sir.'

'Very well,' said the Admiral. 'Fetch me my red shirt.'

Again the danger passed but the lookout was curious as to why the Admiral always asked for his red shirt when battle was imminent.

'It's a question of morale,' explained the Admiral. 'If I'm wounded while wearing a red shirt, the men won't see the blood and will continue to fight.'

When this answer was relayed to the crew, they all agreed that their Admiral was an extremely courageous man.

The following morning the Admiral was relaxing in his quarters when the lookout burst in. 'Twenty enemy ships spotted on the horizon, sir.'

'Very well,' said the Admiral. 'Fetch me my brown underpants.'

Bars

A man walked into a pub and saw a lion serving behind the bar.

'What's the problem?' asked the lion, aware that he was being stared at. 'Have you never seen a lion serving drinks before?'

'It's not that,' said the man. 'I just never thought the gorilla would sell this place.'

A toupee walked into a bar and asked for a drink.

The bartender said: 'I'm not serving you – you're off your head.'

A man walked into a bar and asked for a shot of brake fluid.

'Brake fluid?' said the bartender, shocked. 'We don't serve brake fluid.'

'Oh,' said the man. 'I drink it every day at the garage where I work.'

'You must be crazy!' said the bartender. 'You shouldn't drink brake fluid. It's poisonous. You've got to give it up.'

'Don't worry,' said the man. 'I can stop any time.'

A man was sitting at a bar for half an hour, just staring at his drink. Then a big bruiser of a truck driver sat down next to him, took the drink from the guy and downed it in one. The poor man started crying.

The truck driver felt ashamed of his behaviour and said: 'Come on, man, I was just joking. Here, I'll buy you another drink. I just can't stand seeing a man crying.'

The man said: 'No, it's not that. Today has been the worst day of my life. First I fell asleep and was late for work. My boss, in a rage, fired me. Then when I left the building to get to my car, I discovered it had been stolen. The police said they could do nothing. I got a taxi to return home and when I got out, I remembered I'd left my wallet and credit cards in there. The cab driver just drove away. I went home and found my wife sleeping with the gardener. I left home and came to this bar. And when I was thinking about putting an end to my miserable life, you show up and drink my poison.'

Did you hear about the bailiff who moonlighted as a bartender?
—He served subpoena coladas.

The Lone Ranger and Tonto were at the bar drinking when in walked a cowboy who yelled: 'Whose white horse is that outside?'

The Lone Ranger finished off his whisky, slammed down the glass, turned around and said: 'It's my horse. Why do you want to know?'

The cowboy looked at him and said: 'Well, your horse is standing out there in the sun and he don't look too good.'

The Lone Ranger and Tonto ran outside and they saw that Silver was in bad shape, suffering from heat exhaustion. The Lone Ranger moved his horse into the shade and got a bucket of water. He then poured some of the water over the horse and gave the rest to Silver to drink. He then noticed that there wasn't a breeze so he asked Tonto if he would start running around Silver to get some air flowing and perhaps cool him down.

Being a faithful friend, Tonto started running around Silver. The Lone Ranger stood there for a bit but realized there was not much more he could do, so he went back into the bar and ordered another whiskey.

After a bit, another cowboy walked in and said: 'Whose white horse is that outside?'

Slowly the Lone Ranger turned around and said: 'That is my horse. What's wrong with him now?'

'Nothing,' replied the cowboy. 'I just wanted to let you know that you left your Injun running.'

A man went into a bar but was alarmed to see that all the customers had nasty skin rashes. He asked the bartender: 'Why is everyone here covered in rashes and blisters?'

The bartender replied: 'This is a shingles bar.'

John was sitting outside his local bar one day, enjoying a quiet beer and generally feeling good about himself, when a nun suddenly appeared at his table and started decrying the evils of drink. 'You should be ashamed of yourself, young man!' she ranted. 'Drinking is a sin! Alcohol is the blood of the devil!'

John was pretty annoyed about this and asked her: 'How do you know this, Sister?'

'My Mother Superior told me so,' she answered.

'But have you ever had a drink yourself?' asked John. 'How can you be sure that what you are saying is right?'

The nun was offended and said: 'Don't be ridiculous – of course I have never taken alcohol myself.'

'Then let me buy you a drink,' said John, 'and if you still believe afterwards that it is evil I promise that I will give up drink for life.'

'How could I, a nun, sit outside this bar drinking?' she demanded.

'No problem,' said John. 'I'll get the barman to put your drink in a teacup, then no one will ever know.'

The nun reluctantly agreed, so John went inside to place his order. 'Another beer for me, and a triple vodka on the rocks,' he said to the barman. He lowered his voice then added: 'And could you put the vodka in a teacup?'

The barman replied: 'Oh no! It's not that nun again, is it?'

A skeleton walked into a bar and said: 'I'd like a beer – and a mop.'

A man walked into a bar and ordered a beer. He took his first sip and set it down. While he was looking around the bar, a monkey swung down and stole the pint of beer from him before he was able to react.

The man asked the barman who owned the monkey. The barman replied that the monkey belonged to the bar's piano player.

The man walked over to the piano player and said: 'Do you know your monkey stole my beer?'

The pianist replied: 'No, but if you hum it, I'll play it.'

A man walked into a bar one night and asked for a beer.

'Certainly, sir, that will be one penny,' said the barman.

'One penny?!' exclaimed the guy incredulously.

The barman replied: 'Yes, one penny.'

The man decided he was hungry and glanced over at the menu. He asked the bartender: 'Could I have a nice juicy T-bone steak, with fries, peas and a salad?'

'Certainly, sir,' replied the bartender. 'But all that comes to real money.'

'How much money?' inquired the customer.

'Ten pence,' the barman replied.

'Only ten pence?!' exclaimed the man. 'Where's the guy who owns this place?'

The barman answered: 'Upstairs with my wife.'

'What's he doing with your wife?'

The bartender said: 'The same as what I'm doing to his business!'

An unhappy wife was complaining about her husband spending all his free time in a bar, so one night he took her along with him.

'What would you like?' he asked her.

'Oh, I don't know. The same as you, I suppose,' she answered.

So, the husband ordered a couple of Bourbons and threw his down in one shot. His wife watched him, then took a sip from her glass and immediately spat it out.

'Yuck, that's terrible!' she spluttered. 'I don't know how you can drink this stuff!'

'Well, there you go,' cried the husband. 'And you think I'm out enjoying myself every night!'

Shakespeare walked into a bar and asked for a beer.

'I can't serve you,' said the bartender. 'You're bard.'

A man walked into a bar and sat himself on a stool. The bartender looked at him and asked: 'What'll it be, pal?'

The man said: 'Set me up with seven whisky shots and make them doubles.'

The bartender poured the drinks and watched the man slug one down, then the next, then the next, and so on until all seven were gone almost as quickly as they were served. Staring in disbelief, the bartender asked the man why he was drinking so quickly.

'You'd drink them this fast too if you had what I have,' the man answered.

Curious, the bartender asked: 'Why, what do you have, pal?'

The man replied: 'A quid.'

A man walked into a bar after work and ordered a beer. As he started drinking his beer, he heard a female voice saying seductively: 'You've got nice hair.' The man looked all around him but couldn't see where the voice came from.

A minute later he heard the same voice saying: 'You are a handsome devil.' Again, the man looked around but there were no females nearby, just a bowl of peanuts.

He then walked over to the jukebox to put on a couple of songs. He heard a male voice say: 'Your shoes are horrible.'

The man looked around but there was nobody nearby. He carried on choosing music and again heard the same male voice say: 'Your breath smells terrible.' He looked around but still could not work out where the voices were coming from. He was really puzzled by this so he asked the barman what was going on.

The barman replied: 'Oh, don't worry. The nuts are complimentary and the jukebox is out of order.'

Solution to all of your drinking troubles:

Symptom: Drinking fails to give satisfaction and taste; shirt front is wet.
Fault: Mouth not open or glass being applied to wrong part of face.
Solution: Buy another pint and practice in front of a mirror. Continue with as many pints as necessary until drinking technique is perfect.

Symptom: Drinking fails to give satisfaction and taste; beer unusually pale and clear.
Fault: Glass is empty.
Solution: Find someone who will buy you another pint.

Symptom: Feet cold and wet.
Fault: Glass being held at incorrect angle.
Solution: Turn glass so that open end is pointing at ceiling.

Symptom: Feet warm and wet.
Fault: Loss of self-control.
Solution: Go and stand beside nearest dog – after a while complain to its owner about its lack of house training.

Symptom: Bar blurred.
Fault: You are looking through the bottom of your empty glass.
Solution: Find someone who will buy you another pint.

Symptom: Bar swaying.
Fault: Air turbulence unusually high – maybe due to darts match in progress.
Solution: Insert broom handle down back of jacket.

Symptom: Bar moving.
Fault: You are being carried out.
Solution: Find out if you are being taken to another bar – if not complain loudly that you are being hijacked.

Symptom: The opposite wall is covered in ceiling tiles and has a fluorescent strip across it.
Fault: You have fallen over backwards.
Solution: If glass is still full, and no one is standing on your drinking arm, stay put. If not, get someone to lift you up and lash you to the bar.

Symptom: Everything has gone dim and you have a mouth full of teeth and dog-ends.
Fault: You have fallen over forwards.
Solution: Same as for falling over backwards.

Symptom: You have woken up to find your bed cold, hard and wet. You cannot see your bedroom walls or ceiling.
Fault: You have spent the night in the gutter.
Solution: Check your watch to see if it's opening time – if not treat yourself to a lie-in.

Symptom: Everything has gone dim.
Fault: The pub is closing.
Solution: Panic.

A man walked into a bar but instead of buying a drink he stopped to talk to all of the customers. As he finished with each group of people, they all got up and went to stand outside the window, looking in. Finally, the bar was empty except for this man and the bartender.

The man then strolled up to the bar and said to the bartender: 'I bet you two hundred quid that I can spray beer from my mouth into a shot glass from thirty feet away and not get any outside the glass.'

The bartender thought this guy was crazy but he wanted his two hundred pounds so he agreed. The bartender got out a shot glass, paced off thirty feet, and the contest began.

The man sprayed beer all over the bar. He didn't even touch the shot glass.

When he finished, the bartender looked at him and said: 'Well, I guess you owe me two hundred pounds then!'

The man replied: 'Yeah, but I bet all of those people outside the window fifty quid apiece that you would let me come in here and spray beer all over the bar!'

A man had recently moved to the town and walked into a bar near his house for the first time. He ordered a drink and sat down. Nearby, some of the old-timers were telling jokes.

One of them said, 'Seventeen' and the other old-timers all roared with laughter.

A little later, another of them said, 'Thirty-two' and again, they all laughed and hollered.

Well, the new guy couldn't figure out what was going on, so he asked one of the locals next to him: 'What are these old-timers doing?'

The local answered: 'Well, they've been hanging around together for so long now, they all know the same jokes, so to save extra talking they've given all the jokes numbers.'

The new fellow was impressed and said: 'That's mighty clever! I think I'll try that.'

So he stood up and said in a loud voice: 'Nineteen!'

He was greeted with complete silence – everybody just looked at him but nobody laughed. Embarrassed, he sat down again and asked the local fellow: 'What happened? Why didn't anyone laugh?'

The local replied: 'Well, son, you just didn't tell it right ...'

Vincent Van Gogh walked into a bar.

The bartender said: 'Would you like a drink?'

Van Gogh said: 'No, I've got one 'ere.'

A man walked into a bar with a length of tarmac under his arm.

'What'll you have?' asked the bartender.

The man said, 'I'll have a beer – and one for the road.'

A man walked up to a bar with an ostrich behind him and, as he sat down, the bartender asked for his order.

The man said: 'I'll have a beer.' He then turned to the ostrich and asked: 'What about you?'

'I'll have a beer, too,' said the ostrich.

The bartender poured the beers and said: 'That will be nine pounds fifty, please.'

The man reached into his pocket and paid with the exact change.

The next day, the man and the ostrich came into the bar again, and the man said: 'I'll have a beer.'

The ostrich said: 'I'll have the same.'

Once again the man reached into his pocket and paid with the exact change.

This became a routine until late one evening, the two entered the bar again.

'The usual?' asked the bartender.

'Well, it's close to last orders, so I'll have a large Scotch,' said the man.

'Same for me,' said the ostrich.

'That will be fifteen pounds fifty,' said the bartender.

As was his custom, the man pulled the exact change out of his pocket and placed it on the bar.

The bartender couldn't hold back his curiosity any longer. He asked the man: 'Excuse me, sir. How do you manage to always come up with the exact change out of your pocket every time?'

'Well,' explained the man, 'several years ago I was cleaning the attic and I found this old lamp. When I rubbed it a genie appeared and offered me two wishes. My first wish was that if I ever needed to pay for anything, I could just put my hand in my pocket and the right amount of money would be there.'

'That's brilliant!' exclaimed the bartender. 'Most people would wish for a million pounds or something but you'll always be as rich as you want for as long as you live!'

'That's right!' said the man. 'Whether it's a pint of milk or a Rolls-Royce, the exact money is always there.'

'Amazing!' said the bartender. 'You're a genius! One other thing, sir, what's with the ostrich?'

The man replied: 'Oh, my second wish was for a chick with long legs.'

Battle of the Sexes

MEN

A man walked into a therapist's office, looking really depressed.

'Doctor, you've got to help me,' he said. 'I can't go on like this.'

'What's the problem?' asked the therapist.

'Well, I'm thirty-eight years old and I still have no luck with the ladies. No matter how hard I try, I just seem to scare them away.'

'My friend,' said the therapist, 'this isn't a serious problem. You just need to work on your self-esteem. Each morning, I want you to get up and go straight to your bathroom mirror. Tell yourself that you are a good person, a fun person and an attractive person. But you must say it with real conviction. Within a week you'll have women buzzing all around you.'

The man seemed content with this advice and walked out intent on putting it into practice. Three weeks later he returned to the therapist wearing the same downtrodden expression on his face.

'Didn't my advice work?' inquired the therapist.

'It worked all right,' said the man. 'For the past three weeks I've enjoyed some of the best moments of my life with the most fabulous looking women.'

'So what's your problem?'

'I don't have a problem,' the man replied. 'My wife does!'

Adam said to God: 'When you created Eve, why did you make her body so curvy and tender, unlike mine?'

God replied: 'I did that, Adam, so that you could love her.'

'And why,' asked Adam, 'did you give her long, shiny, beautiful hair, but not me?'

'So that you could love her,' answered God.

'Then why did you make her so stupid?' asked Adam. 'Certainly not so that I could love her?'

'No, Adam,' said God. 'I did that so that she could love you.'

What a woman wants in a man (original list)
Handsome
Charming
Financially successful
A caring listener
Witty
In good shape
Dresses with style
Appreciates the finer things in life
Full of thoughtful surprises
An imaginative, romantic lover

What a woman wants in a man (revised list)
Not too ugly
Doesn't belch or scratch his ass in public
Steady worker
Doesn't nod off during conversations
Can remember jokes from Christmas crackers
Is in good enough shape to rearrange the
    furniture
Usually wears matching socks
Knows not to buy champagne with screw-top lids
Remembers to put the toilet seat lid down
Shaves at weekends

What's the difference between men and women?
—A woman wants one man to satisfy her every need;
a man wants every woman to satisfy his one need.

Why are men like noodles?
—They're always in hot water, they lack taste and
they need dough.

Why do men buy electric lawn mowers?
—So that they can find their way back to the house.

What's the quickest way to a man's heart?
—Straight through the ribcage.

Why do men whistle while they're sitting on the
toilet?
—It helps them remember which end they need to
wipe.

What has eight arms and an IQ of sixty?
—Four men watching a football game.

Advice to daughters about men:

Don't imagine you can change him, unless he's in nappies.

The best way to get a man to do something is suggest he's too old for it.

Love is blind – but marriage is a real eye-opener.

If you want a committed man – look in a mental hospital.

The Children of Israel wandered around the desert for forty years. Even in Biblical times, men wouldn't ask for directions.

A sense of humour doesn't mean you tell him jokes – it means you laugh at his.

Sadly, all men are created equal.

UNDERSTANDING MEN:

'It's a guy thing.'
Translation: 'There is no rational thought pattern connected with it, and you have no chance at all of making it logical.'

'Can I help with dinner?'
Translation: 'Why isn't it on the table?'

'It would take too long to explain.'
Translation: 'I have no idea how it works.'

'I was listening to you. It's just that I have things on my mind.'
Translation: 'That girl standing over there is a real babe.'

'Take a break honey, you're working too hard.'
Translation: 'I can't hear the game over the vacuum cleaner.'

'That's interesting, dear.'
Translation: 'Are you still talking?'

'I was just thinking about you and got you these roses.'

Translation: 'The girl selling them on the corner was a real babe.'

'Oh, don't fuss – I just cut myself, it's no big deal.'

Translation: 'I have actually severed a limb but will bleed to death before I admit I'm hurt.'

'I can't find it!'

Translation: 'It didn't fall straight into my outstretched hands, so I'm completely clueless.'

'You look terrific!'

Translation: 'Oh, please don't try on another outfit, I'm starving.'

'We're not lost! I know exactly where we are.'

Translation: 'No one will ever see us alive again.'

'You know I could never love anyone else.'

Translation: 'I am used to the way you yell at me and realize that it could be worse.'

'Uh huh,' 'Sure, honey,' or 'Yes, dear.'

Translation: Absolutely nothing. It's a conditioned response.

'I heard you.'
Translation: 'I haven't the foggiest clue what you just said and I'm hoping desperately that I can fake it well enough so that you don't spend the next three days yelling at me.'

'You know how bad my memory is.'
Translation: 'I can remember the theme tune of every Bond movie, the address of the first girl I ever kissed and the score of every match my team played for the past thirty years, but I forgot our anniversary.'

'What did I do this time?'
Translation: 'What did you catch me at?'

What's the difference between a man and childbirth?
—One can be really painful and almost unbearable while the other is just having a baby.

What's one thing that all men in singles bars have in common?
—They're married.

How do men sort their laundry?
—'Filthy' and 'Filthy but Wearable'.

Everybody on Earth died and went to heaven. On their arrival, God announced that he wanted the men to form two lines – one for all the men who had dominated their women on Earth, the other for all the men who had been dominated by their women. Then he told the women to go with St Peter. When God turned round, he saw that the men had indeed formed two lines. The men who had been dominated by their women stretched back a hundred miles whereas the line of men who had dominated their women consisted of just one person.

God was furious. 'You should be ashamed of yourselves for having been so weak,' he boomed. 'Only one of my sons has been strong. He is the only man of whom I am truly proud.'

God turned to the man who was standing alone. 'Tell me, my son, how did you manage to be the only one in this line?'

'I'm not sure,' replied the man meekly. 'My wife told me to stand here.'

How do you scare a man?
—Creep up behind him and start throwing rice.

What makes a man think about a candlelit dinner?
—A power cut.

What's the difference between Government bonds and men?
—Bonds mature.

A man had seven children and was so proud of his virility that, despite his wife's objections, he constantly referred to her both in private and in public as 'mother of seven'.

One evening the couple went to a party. When the husband was ready to go home, he called out loudly: 'Shall we leave now, Mother of Seven?'

Annoyed by his lack of discretion, his wife shouted back: 'Ready when you are, Father of Four.'

The Different Qualities of Men and Women:

Women are honest, loyal and forgiving. They are smart, knowing that knowledge is power. But they still know how to use their softer side to make a point. Women want to do the best for their family, their friends and themselves. Their hearts break when a friend dies. They have sorrow at the loss of a family member, yet they are strong when they think there is no strength left. A woman can make a romantic evening unforgettable. Women drive, fly, walk, run or e-mail you to show how much they care about you. Women do more than just give birth. They bring joy and hope. They give compassion and ideals. They provide moral support to their family and friends. And all they want back is a hug and a smile. The heart of a woman is what makes the world spin.

Men are good at lifting heavy stuff and killing spiders.

WOMEN

Female version:
First woman: 'Oh, you got a haircut! That's so cute!'

Second woman: 'Do you think so? I wasn't sure when she gave me the mirror. I mean, you don't think it's too fluffy-looking?'

First woman: 'Oh God, no! It's perfect. I'd love to get my hair cut like that but I think my face is too wide. I'm pretty much stuck with how it is, I think.'

Second woman: 'Are you serious? I think your face is adorable. And you could easily get one of those layer cuts – that would really suit you. I was going to do that except that I was afraid it would accentuate my long neck.'

First woman: 'What's wrong with your neck? I would love to have a neck like yours: anything to take the attention away from my awful shoulder line.'

Second woman: 'Are you kidding? I know girls that would love to have your shoulders. Everything hangs so well on you. You're like a walking fashion catalogue. But look at my arms – see how short they are? If I had your shoulders, I could get clothes to fit me so much easier.'

Male version:
First man: 'Haircut?'
Second man: 'Yeah!'

Two men were admiring a famous actress. 'Still,' said one, 'if you take away her fabulous hair, her magnificent breasts, her beautiful eyes, her perfect features and her stunning figure, what are you left with?'

The other replied: 'My wife.'

A woman was sitting at a bar enjoying some after-work cocktails with her girlfriends when a tall, handsome young man walked in. He was so good-looking that the woman could not take her eyes off him. After a few minutes, he noticed that she was gazing adoringly at him and went over to talk to her. Before she could apologize for staring, he said to her: 'I'll do anything, absolutely anything, that you want me to do, no matter how kinky, for fifty pounds on one condition.'

'What's that?' asked the woman.

The young man replied: 'You have to tell me what you want me to do in just three words.'

The woman considered his proposition for a moment, took out her purse and counted out five ten-pound notes, which she pressed into the young man's hand along with her address. Then she looked into his eyes and purred seductively: 'Clean my house.'

A police officer knocked on the door of a man's house and said solemnly: 'It looks like your wife's been in a really nasty accident.'

'Yes, I know,' said the husband, 'but she's got a lovely personality.'

A man was walking through the woods when he stumbled across a lamp. In time-honoured tradition, he picked it up, rubbed it and out popped a genie who granted him three wishes.

'I'd like a million pounds,' said the man. And POOF! A million pounds appeared.

'And what is your second wish?' asked the genie.

'I'd like a new Ferrari,' said the man. And POOF! A gleaming new Ferrari suddenly appeared.

'And for your third wish?' asked the genie.

'I'd like to be irresistible to women,' replied the man.

And POOF! He was turned into a box of chocolates.

WOMEN'S DICTIONARY

Argument – *n*. A discussion that occurs when you're right but he just hasn't realized it yet.

Airhead – *n*. What a woman intentionally becomes when pulled over by a traffic cop.

Barbecue – *n*. You bought the groceries, washed the lettuce, sliced the tomatoes, chopped the onions, marinated the meat and cleaned everything up, but he 'made the dinner'.

Childbirth – *n*. You go through thirty-six hours of excruciating contractions; he gets to hold your hand and say 'focus … breathe … push'.

Clothes dryer – *n*. An appliance designed to eat socks.

Diet drink – *n*. Something you buy at a late-night shop to go with a half-pound bag of peanut M&Ms.

Exercise – *n*. To walk up and down a shopping mall, occasionally resting to make a purchase.

Grocery list – *n*. What you spend half an hour writing, then forget to take with you to the supermarket.

Hairdresser – *n.* Someone who is able to create a style you will never be able to duplicate again.

Lipstick – *n.* On your lips, colouring to enhance the beauty of your mouth. On his collar, colouring only a tramp would wear.

Valentine's Day – *n.* A day when you dream of a candlelit dinner, diamonds and romance but are lucky if you get a card.

Waterproof mascara – *n.* Comes off if you cry, shower or swim but will not come off if you try to remove it.

What do you call a woman with a screwdriver in one hand, a knife in the other, a pair of scissors between the toes on her left foot and a corkscrew between the toes on her right foot?
—A Swiss army wife.

Romance Mathematics:
Smart man + Smart woman = Romance
Smart man + Dumb woman = Affair
Dumb man + Smart woman = Marriage
Dumb man + Dumb woman = Pregnancy

UNDERSTANDING WOMEN:

'We need to talk.'
Translation: 'I need to complain.'

'Sure, go ahead.'
Translation: 'I don't want you to.'

'I'm not yelling!'
Translation: 'Yes, I am yelling because I think it's important.'

'We need.'
Translation: 'I want.'

'It's your decision.'
Translation: 'The correct decision should be obvious by now.'

'Do what you want.'
Translation: 'You'll pay for this later.'

'I'm not upset.'
Translation: 'Of course I'm upset, you moron!'

'You're … so manly.'
Translation: 'You need a shave and a shower.'

'You're certainly attentive tonight.'
Translation: 'Is sex all you think about?'

'I'm not emotional and I'm not over-reacting.'
Translation: 'I've got my period.'

'Be romantic, turn out the light.'
Translation: 'I have flabby thighs.'

'I want new curtains.'
Translation: 'And carpeting, and furniture, and wallpaper.'

'I need new wedding shoes.'
Translation: 'The other forty pairs are the wrong shade of white.'

'Hang the picture there.'
Translation: 'No, I mean hang it there!'

'I heard a noise.'
Translation: 'I noticed you were almost asleep.'

'Do you love me?'
Translation: 'I'm going to ask for something expensive.'

'How much do you love me?'
Translation: 'I did something today that you're really not going to like.'

'I'll be ready in a minute.'
Translation: 'Kick off your shoes and find a good game on TV.'

'Is my bum fat?'
Translation: 'Tell me I'm beautiful.'

'You have to learn to communicate.'
Translation: 'Just agree with me.'

'Are you listening to me?'
Translation: 'Too late, you're dead.'

'Yes.'
Translation: 'No.'

'No.'
Translation: 'No.'

'Maybe.'
Translation: 'No.'

'I'm sorry.'
Translation: 'You'll be sorry.'

'This kitchen is so inconvenient.'
Translation: 'I want a new house.'

'Do you like this recipe?'
Translation: 'It's so easy to fix, so you'd better get used to it.'

'Was that the baby?'
Translation: 'Why don't you get out of bed and walk him until he goes to sleep?'

'All we're going to buy is a soap dish.'
Translation: 'It goes without saying that we're stopping at the cosmetics department, the shoe department, and I need to look at a few purses, and those blue sheets would look great in the bedroom, and did you bring your chequebook?'

With a plane about to crash into a mountain, a female passenger stood up and shouted: 'If I'm going to die, I want to die feeling like a woman.' Then she took off her top and cried: 'Is there anyone on this plane who is man enough to make me feel like a woman?'

Hearing this, a man stood up, took off his shirt and said: 'Iron this, love.'

Two men were propped up against the bar at the end of a heavy drinking session. 'Tell me,' said one. 'Have you ever gone to bed with a really ugly woman?'

'No,' replied the other. 'But I've woken up with plenty!'

A woman worries about the future until she gets a husband.

A man never worries about the future until he gets a wife.

A successful man is one who earns more money than his wife can spend.

A successful woman is one who can find such a man.

To be happy with a man, you must understand him a lot and love him a little.

To be happy with a woman you must love her a lot and try not to understand her at all.

Two women were out on a shopping expedition when they came across a new department store that advertised men for sale.

The sign on the first floor read: 'All the men on this floor are short and ugly.' So the women decided to take the elevator to the second floor.

The sign on the second floor read: 'All the men on this floor are short and handsome.' Still unimpressed, the women continued up the elevator to the next floor.

The sign on the third floor read: 'All the men on this floor are tall and ugly.' The two women didn't like the sound of that, so they kept going.

The sign on the fourth floor read: 'All the men on this floor are tall and handsome.' The two women were excited at the prospect but decided to see what was on the fifth and final floor.

There they found a sign that read: 'There are no men here. This floor was built to prove there's just no way of pleasing a woman.'

What's the difference between a battery and a woman?
—A battery has a positive side.

Birds

A man with a talking parrot was getting married. On the day of his wedding he warned the parrot: 'Now listen to me. I know you are always sat in that window sticking your beak in, but when my new wife and I get back from our wedding I want you to turn around so that we can have a spot of privacy. And no matter what you hear, I do not want you to turn back. If you do, I'll break your neck. Understand?'

The parrot reluctantly agreed.

When the couple returned from the wedding, the parrot turned around as ordered and behind him the bride and groom started to pack for their honeymoon. However the bride had packed too much and they couldn't get the suitcase closed.

'Get on top and sit on it, honey,' advised the groom.

She did so, but even after grunting and groaning she still couldn't shut the case.

'You get on top, baby, it might be better,' suggested the bride.

So the groom grunted and groaned and tried his best but he still couldn't shut the case.

After a little thought, the groom said: 'I know. We'll both get on top and see if that's any better.'

The parrot turned around and said: 'Neck or no neck, I have to see this!'

An elderly woman was looking for a pet that would be a good companion and not much trouble. The pet store owner suggested a parrot, showed it to her and guaranteed that it would be a wonderful companion. The woman asked if it would behave if she took it to church with her on Sundays. The owner said it shouldn't be a problem and that she could put the parrot on her shoulder and it would stay there.

So she bought the parrot and spent the next week getting to know it. Assured that it spoke properly and was well behaved, she put it on her shoulder and went off to church. Just as everyone fell silent and the sermon began, the parrot looked around, squawked and said: 'It's goddamned cold in here!'

When everyone turned to look at the woman, she ran out of the church in total embarrassment. Throughout the next week, she talked to the parrot and explained the need to remain quiet during church. The parrot understood so she put it on her shoulder and went to church the following Sunday.

Once again, just as everything fell quiet and the sermon began, the parrot squawked, looked around and loudly proclaimed: 'It's goddamned cold in here!'

The red-faced woman ran from the church, her reputation in shreds.

The next day she returned to the pet store and explained the embarrassing situation to the owner. Since she didn't want to get rid of the parrot, the owner suggested the following solution: 'If the parrot does that again, grab it by the legs, swing it around five or six times and return it to your shoulder.'

'Will that work?' asked the woman.

'Guaranteed!' exclaimed the owner.

So the next Sunday she took the parrot to church and, sure enough, just as the sermon started, the parrot squawked: 'It's goddamned cold in here!'

The woman immediately grabbed the bird's legs, swung it around five or six times and placed it back on her shoulder.

The parrot shook its head, ruffled its feathers and said: 'Pretty bloody windy, too!'

A lady approached her local priest and told him: 'Father, I have these two talking female parrots, but they only know how to say one thing: "Hi, we're prostitutes. Do you want to have some fun?"'

'That's terrible!' the priest exclaimed. 'But I have a solution to your problem. You can put them with my two male talking parrots. I taught them to read the Bible and pray the rosary.'

So the lady brought over her parrots and put them in the priest's cage with his two male parrots.

'Hi, we're prostitutes. Do you want to have some fun?' squawked the females.

One male parrot looked over at the other and exclaimed: 'Put the beads away. Our prayers have been answered!'

A young man's mother lived in Miami Beach and he didn't see her that often. His father was no longer around and he was worried that his mother was lonely, so for her birthday he bought her a rare parrot, trained to speak seven languages. He had a courier deliver the bird to his mother and a few days later he called her to see how she was getting along with her new pet.

'What do you think of the bird?' he asked.

'The bird was good, but a little tough,' she replied. 'I should have cooked it longer.'

'You ate the bird? Ma, the bird was very expensive. It spoke seven languages!'

'Oh, excuse me. But, if the bird was so smart, why didn't it say something when I put it in the oven?'

Kelly had a pet parrot, but the bird would embarrass her whenever she came into the apartment with a man. He would shout all kinds of obscenities, always leading off with: 'Somebody's gonna get it tonight!' In desperation, Kelly went to her local pet shop and explained her parrot problem to the pet shop proprietor.

'What you need,' he said, 'is a female parrot, too. I don't have one in stock, but I'll order one. Meanwhile, you could borrow this female owl until the female parrot arrives.'

Kelly took the owl home and put it near her parrot. It was immediately obvious that the parrot didn't care for the owl and kept glaring at it. That night, Kelly wasn't her usual nervous self as she opened the door to bring her gentleman friend in for a nightcap, but then suddenly she heard the parrot screech and she knew that things hadn't changed.

'Somebody's gonna get it tonight! Somebody's gonna get it tonight!' the parrot said.

The owl said: 'Who? Who?'

And the parrot said: 'Not you, big eyes!'

Scientists had long been curious about why no penguin corpses were found on the ice pack. What happened to their bodies when they died?

The mystery was recently solved.

It turned out that the penguin was a very ritualistic bird and lived an extremely ordered and complex life. The penguin was very committed to its family, generally mated for life and usually maintained contact with its offspring throughout its existence.

Whenever a penguin was found dead on the ice surface, members of the family and social circle dug a hole in the ice, using their vestigial wings and beaks. The male penguins then gathered in a circle around the fresh grave and sang: 'Freeze a jolly good fellow. Freeze a jolly good fellow.' Then they kicked him in the ice hole.

How do penguins drink their cola?
—On the rocks.

What's black and white and goes round and around?
—A penguin in a revolving door.

Why don't you see penguins in Britain?
—Because they're afraid of Wales.

Who is a penguin's favourite pop star?
—Seal.

Why don't penguins like rock music?
—They only like sole.

Why do penguins carry fish in their beaks?
—Because they haven't got any pockets.

An old farmer decided it was time to get a new rooster for his hens. The current rooster was still doing a reasonable job, but he was starting to show his age. So the farmer bought a young cock from the local rooster emporium and turned him loose in the barnyard.

Well, the old rooster saw the young one strutting around and got a little worried. 'They're trying to replace me,' he thought. 'I've got to do something about this.'

So he walked up to the new bird and said: 'I understand you're the new stud in town? I bet you really think you're hot stuff, don't you? Well, I'm not ready for the chopping block yet. I bet I'm still the better bird. And to prove it, I challenge you to a race around that hen house over there. We'll run around it ten times and whoever finishes first gets to have all the hens for himself.'

The young rooster was a proud sort and he definitely thought he was more than a match for the old guy. 'You're on,' said the young rooster. 'And since I know I'm so great, I'll even give you a head start of half a lap. I'll still win easily.'

So the two roosters went over to the hen house to start the race with all the hens gathered around to watch. The race began and the hens started cheering the roosters on. After the first lap, the old rooster was still maintaining his lead. After the second lap, the old guy's lead had slipped a little but he was still hanging in there. Unfortunately, the old rooster's lead continued to slip each time around.

By now the farmer had heard all the commotion. He dashed into the house, grabbed his shotgun and ran out to the barnyard figuring a fox or something was after his chickens. When he got there, he saw the two roosters running around the hen house, with the old rooster still slightly in the lead. He immediately took his shotgun, aimed, fired, and blew the young rooster away.

As he returned to the house, the farmer muttered to himself: 'Damn, that's the third gay rooster I've bought this month!'

A duck walked into a bar and ordered a pint of beer and a ham sandwich.

The barman looked at him and said: 'Hang on! You're a duck.'

'I see your eyes are working,' replied the duck.

'And you can talk!' exclaimed the barman.

'I see your ears are working, too,' said the duck sarcastically. 'Now if you don't mind, can I have my beer and my sandwich, please?'

'Certainly. Sorry about that,' said the barman as he pulled the duck's pint. 'It's just we don't get many ducks in this bar. What are you doing round this way?'

'I'm working on the building site across the road,' explained the duck. 'I'm a plasterer.'

The flabbergasted barman could not believe what the duck was saying and wanted to learn more, but took the hint when the duck pulled out a newspaper from his bag and proceeded to read it.

So the duck read his paper, drank his beer, ate his sandwich and left the bar. The same thing happened every day for the next two weeks.

Then one day the circus arrived in town. The ringmaster came into the bar for a beer and the barman said to him: 'You're with the circus, aren't you? Well, I know this duck that could be just brilliant in your circus. He talks, drinks beer, eats sandwiches, reads the newspaper and everything!'

'Sounds marvellous,' said the ringmaster, handing over his business card. 'Get him to give me a call.'

So the next day when the duck came into the pub, the barman said: 'Hey Mr Duck, I reckon I can line you up with a top job, paying really good money.'

'I'm always looking for the next job,' said the duck. 'Where is it?'

'At the circus,' answered the barman.

'The circus?' repeated the duck.

'That's right,' said the barman.

'The circus?' the duck asked again. 'That place with the big tent?'

'Yeah,' the barman said.

'With all the animals who live in cages, and performers who live in caravans?' said the duck.

'Of course,' the barman replied.

'And the tent has canvas sides and a big canvas roof with a hole in the middle?' persisted the duck.

'That's right!' answered the barman.

The duck shook his head in amazement and said: 'What the hell would they want with a plasterer?'

A pheasant was standing in a field chatting with a bull. 'I would love to be able to get to the top of that tree over yonder,' sighed the pheasant, 'but I haven't got the energy.'

'Well, why don't you nibble on some of my droppings?' replied the bull. 'They're packed with nutrients.'

So the pheasant pecked at a lump of dung and found that it actually gave him enough strength to reach the first branch of the tree. The next day, after eating some more, he reached the second branch. And from there he was eventually able to reach the very top of the tree.

However, he was then spotted by a farmer who dashed into the farmhouse, emerged with a shotgun and shot the pheasant right out of the tree.

The moral of the story: Bullshit might get you to the top, but it won't keep you there.

Birth

For his school science homework an eight-year-old boy was told to write about childbirth.

So that evening he asked his mother: 'How was I born?'

'Well, uh,' said the mother, embarrassed, 'the stork brought you.'

'Oh,' said the boy. 'And how did you and Dad get born?'

'The stork brought us, too,' replied the mother uneasily.

'What about Grandma and Grandpa?'

'The stork brought them as well.'

'Okay,' said the boy. 'Thanks, Mum.'

The next day he submitted his homework. It began: 'This has been difficult for me to write because I learned that there has not been a natural childbirth in my family for three generations.'

'Will the father be present during the birth?' asked the obstetrician.

'No,' replied the mother-to-be. 'He and my husband don't get along.'

A little boy asked his mother: 'Are the people next door very poor?'

'I don't think so,' said the mother. 'Why do you ask?'

'Because they made such a fuss when their baby swallowed a penny.'

Shortly after giving birth to her eleventh baby, a woman bumped into her parish priest. He congratulated her on the new addition to the family but added: 'Isn't eleven babies a bit much?'

'Well, Father,' she said, 'I don't know why I get pregnant so often. It must be something in the air.'

'Yes,' said the priest. 'Your legs!'

Desperate for a baby, a Catholic couple asked their priest to pray for them.

'Very well,' said the priest. 'I'm going to Rome next week for several months, so I shall light a candle for you at the altar of St Peter.'

Nine months later, the priest heard that the wife had given birth to sextuplets. He rushed off to see her but was surprised that there was no sign of her husband.

'Where is he?' asked the priest. 'I thought he'd have been with you at a time such as this.'

'No, Father,' explained the woman. 'He's gone to Rome to blow out your bloody candle!'

A woman phoned her mother from hospital with news of her new baby. 'He weighs seven pounds ten ounces and he's the absolute image of his father.'

'Never mind,' said the mother. 'Just so long as he's healthy.'

A husband rushed his heavily pregnant wife to hospital. There, the doctor told them: 'I've invented a new machine that you might like to try. It takes some of the labour pains away from the mother and gives them to the father.'

The couple thought it sounded like a good idea, so the doctor hooked up the machine and put it on a level of twenty per cent of pain switched from the mother to the father. After a while the husband said: 'I feel fine. Why don't you turn it up to a higher level?'

So the doctor turned the machine up to fifty per cent transfer of pain from the mother to the father. 'I'm still not feeling any pain,' said the husband. 'You might as well turn it up to a hundred per cent.'

The doctor warned: 'This much could kill you if you're not prepared.'

'I'm ready,' insisted the husband, and so the doctor turned the machine on to full transfer of pain from the mother to the father.

The husband still didn't feel a thing and twelve hours later the couple left the hospital happy after a pain-free labour. But when they arrived home, they found the mailman dead on the front porch.

BRINGING UP BABY

First baby: You start wearing maternity clothes as soon as your pregnancy is confirmed.
Second baby: You wear your regular clothes for as long as possible.
Third baby: You maternity clothes are your regular clothes.

First baby: You practise your breathing religiously.
Second baby: You don't bother practising because you remember that breathing didn't help at all last time.
Third baby: You ask for an epidural in your eighth month.

First baby: You regularly wash your baby's clothes and keep them in immaculate condition.
Second baby: You throw out only the baby clothes with the darkest stains.
Third baby: What's wrong with boys wearing pink?

First baby: At the first sign of distress, you pick up your baby.
Second baby: You pick up the baby when its crying threatens to wake your firstborn.
Third baby: You teach your three-year-old how to rock the baby.

First baby: You change your baby's nappy every hour, regardless of whether it is necessary.

Second baby: You change the nappy every two to three hours, if needed.

Third baby: You try to change the nappy before neighbours complain about the smell.

First baby: If the baby's dummy falls on the floor, you put it away until you can wash it.

Second baby: If the dummy falls on the floor, you squirt the fluff off with juice from the baby's bottle.

Third baby: If the dummy falls on the floor, you quickly wipe it on your shirt and put it straight back in baby's mouth.

First baby: You spend most of the day just gazing in wonder at your baby.

Second baby: You spend most of the day making sure your older child isn't pinching or prodding the baby.

Third baby: You spend most of the day hiding from the children.

First baby: The first time you leave your baby with a sitter, you call home half a dozen times.

Second baby: Just before you walk out the door, you remember to leave a number where you can be reached.

Third baby: You tell the babysitter to call you only if she sees blood.

First baby: If your first child swallows a coin, you rush it to hospital.
Second baby: If your second child swallows a coin, you wait for the item to be passed naturally.
Third baby: If your third child swallows a coin, you deduct it from his pocket money.

How do you get a baby astronaut to sleep?
—You rock-et.

A woman boarded a bus with her baby. The bus driver said: 'I'm sorry, madam, but that is the ugliest baby I've ever seen in my life.'

Mortified, the woman sat down. As she started sobbing, the man in the next seat asked her what was wrong.

'The driver just insulted me,' she said.

'That's terrible,' replied the man. 'You shouldn't have to put up with that. Here, have a mint to calm your nerves. And here's a banana for the chimp.'

It was many years since the embarrassing day when a young woman, with a baby in her arms, entered the butcher's shop, confronted him with the news that the baby was his and asked what he was going to do about it. Finally he offered to provide her with free meat until the boy was sixteen and she agreed.

He had been counting the years off on his calendar and one day the teenager, who had been collecting the meat each week, came into the shop and said: 'I'll be sixteen tomorrow.'

'I know,' said the butcher with a smile, 'I've been counting too. Tell your mother, when you take this parcel of meat home, that it is the last free meat she'll get and watch the expression on her face.'

When the boy arrived home he told his mother. She laughed and said: 'Son, go back to the butcher and tell him I have also had free bread, free milk, and free groceries for the last sixteen years and watch the expression on his face!'

'I see the baby's nose is running again,' said a worried father.

'For heaven's sake!' snapped his wife. 'Can't you think of anything other than horse racing?'

A three-year-old boy overheard his mother revealing that she was pregnant again. The following week, a family friend asked him if he was excited about having a new brother or sister.

'Yes,' said the boy, 'and I know what we're going to name it. If it's a girl, we're going to call her Laura, and if it's another boy we're going to call it Quits.'

An anxious husband phoned the hospital. 'My wife is pregnant,' he said breathlessly. 'Her contractions are less than two minutes apart.'

'Is this her first child?' asked the nurse.

'No, you silly woman. This is her husband!'

A woman in labour with her first child started to shout over and over again: 'Shouldn't, wouldn't, couldn't, isn't, won't, can't.'

Her husband was worried and asked the doctor: 'What's happening to my wife?'

'Don't worry,' said the doctor. 'She's just having contractions.'

Blondes

A blonde was walking in the country when she came to a river. Seeing another blonde standing on the opposite bank, she shouted: 'How can I get to the other side?'

The second blonde shouted back: 'You are on the other side!'

What can strike a blonde without her even knowing it?
—A thought.

Why do blondes wear earmuffs?
—To avoid the draught.

Three women – a blonde, a brunette and a redhead – worked in an office for the same female boss. Every day the boss left work early and so eventually the three decided that they would start leaving early, too. The brunette wanted to get home and play with her baby son, the redhead wanted to work out at the gym and the blonde wanted to get home to see her husband.

However, when the blonde arrived home, she could hear giggling noises coming from the bedroom. She crept upstairs and peeking through the slightly open door, she was horrified to see her husband in bed with her boss. Without making a sound, she crept back downstairs and out of the house.

The next day at work the brunette and the redhead said they intended to leave early again and asked the blonde whether she was planning to do the same.

'No way,' replied the blonde. 'I almost got caught yesterday!'

A blonde was crossing the road when she got hit by a car. The driver rushed over to check that she was okay.

'I can't see straight,' wailed the blonde. 'Everything seems blurry.'

Leaning over her, the worried driver said: 'How many fingers have I got up?'

'Oh no!' cried the blonde. 'Don't tell me I'm paralysed from the waist down, too!'

Why did the blonde keep a coat-hanger on her back seat?
—In case she locked her keys in the car.

What's the definition of paralysis?
—Four blondes at a crossroads.

Why can't blondes make ice cubes?
—They forget the recipe.

What does a blonde do if she's not in bed by ten o'clock?
—She picks up her bag and goes home.

A blonde waitress was sobbing her heart out. Her boss asked her what was wrong.

'I got a phone call this morning saying that my mother has died,' wailed the blonde.

'I'm sorry to hear that,' said the boss. 'Why don't you take the rest of the day off?'

'It's okay,' said the blonde. 'I'm better off keeping myself occupied here.'

Even so, the boss continued to check on her and was alarmed to see her burst into tears again a few hours later.

'What's up?' he asked.

'It's sooo terrible!' cried the blonde. 'I've just had a phone call from my sister – and her mum has died too!'

An office manager asked his young blonde secretary why she was late for work that morning.

'I'm sorry,' she said, 'but on my way to work I witnessed a road accident and I was first at the scene. It was awful. There were mangled vehicles with bodies inside and there was blood all over the road. But thank goodness that first aid course I went to last year helped – all my training came back to me.'

'What did you do?' asked her boss.

'I sat down and put my head between my legs to stop myself from fainting.'

A blonde went into a library and shouted: 'I'll have a cheeseburger and fries, please.'

The librarian looked at her in disbelief and said: 'Excuse me! This is a library.'

The blonde realized her mistake and whispered: 'I'll have a cheeseburger and fries, please.'

A blonde decided to take up ice fishing. Finding a nice lake, she had just begun cutting a hole in the ice when she heard a distant voice boom: 'You won't find any fish there.'

Puzzled by the mysterious voice, she cut another hole in the ice several feet away. Again the distant voice boomed: 'You won't find any fish there.'

By now seriously spooked, the blonde looked up and asked: 'Are you God?'

'No,' replied the voice. 'I'm the manager of the ice rink!'

A blonde bought an AM radio. It took her a month to figure out she could play it in the afternoon too.

Why did the blonde stare at the carton of orange juice?
—Because it said concentrate.

Why do employers give blondes only forty-five minutes for lunch?
—Because any longer and they'd have to retrain them.

What do you call a blonde with a brain?
—A golden retriever.

How do you get a blonde to marry you?
—Tell her she's pregnant.

What do you call a blonde skeleton in a cupboard?
—The 1989 World Hide-and-Seek Champion.

Why did the blonde go out with her purse open?
—Because she had heard there would be some change in the weather.

Cannibals

What do the guests do at a cannibal wedding?
—They toast the bride and groom.

When do cannibals leave the table?
—When everyone's eaten.

Did you hear about the cannibal who loved fast food?
—He ordered a pizza with everybody on it.

What is a cannibal's favourite type of television show?
—A celebrity roast.

Have you heard about the cannibal restaurant?
—Dinner costs an arm and a leg.

What is a cannibal's favourite game?
—Swallow the leader.

What did the cannibal get when he was late for dinner?
—The cold shoulder.

A father cannibal said to his daughter: 'It's time you got married. We'll start looking for an edible bachelor.'

Two cannibals were eating a clown. One said to the other: 'Does this taste funny to you?'

A man visited his cannibal neighbour to admire his new refrigerator.

'What is the storage capacity?' the man asked.

'I'm not exactly sure,' the cannibal replied. 'But it at least holds the two men that delivered it.'

While walking in the depths of the African jungle, a tourist asked the guide: 'Are we safe? Aren't there cannibals around here?'

The guide said: 'It is perfectly safe. You can be sure there are no cannibals in Africa.'

The tourist was unconvinced and asked: 'But there may be still some cannibals?'

The guide replied: 'No, rest assured. We ate the last one on Monday.'

Two cannibals met one day. The first cannibal said: 'You know, I just can't seem to get a tender missionary. I've baked them, I've roasted them, I've stewed them, I've barbecued them, I've tried every sort of marinade. I just can't seem to get them tender.'

The second cannibal asked: 'What kind of missionary do you use?'

The other replied: 'You know, the ones that hang

97

out at that place at the bend of the river. They have those brown cloaks with a rope around the waist and they're sort of bald on top with a funny ring of hair on their heads.'

'No wonder you've had problems,' the second cannibal replied. 'Those are friars!'

At the site of a plane crash, the lone survivor sat with his back against a tree, chewing on a bone. As he tossed the bone onto a huge pile of other bones, he noticed the rescue team approaching. 'Thank God!' he cried out in relief. 'I am saved!'

The rescue team did not move, as they were in shock at the sight of the pile of human bones beside this lone survivor. Obviously he had eaten his comrades. The survivor saw the horror in their faces and hung his own head in shame.

'You can't judge me for this,' he insisted. 'I had to survive. Is it so wrong to want to live?'

The leader of the rescue team stepped forward, shaking his head in disbelief. He said to the survivor: 'I won't judge you for doing what was necessary to survive but for goodness' sake, your plane only went down yesterday!'

Two ferocious cannibal chiefs sat licking their fingers after a large meal.

'Your wife makes a delicious roast,' said one chief.

'Thanks,' said the other. 'I'm going to miss her.'

The cannibal king was having dinner when a servant came running in. 'Your Majesty,' he said. 'The slaves are revolting!'

'You don't have to tell me,' said the king. 'I'm trying to eat them. Where did we get these slaves anyway?'

'From the country next door,' replied the servant.

'We must get a new butcher,' said the king. 'Bring me the chef.'

'I can't, Your Majesty, she's still cooking for you.'

'Very well,' said the king. 'Bring her to me once she's crispy enough.'

Children

Two children, Ben and Jack, were lying in adjacent hospital beds.

Ben leaned over and asked: 'What are you in here for?'

Jack replied: 'I'm here to have my tonsils removed.'

'I've had that done before,' said Ben, 'and there's nothing to worry about. They put you to sleep and when you wake up they give you ice-cream and cake.'

'What are you in here for?' asked Jack.

'A circumcision,' replied Ben.

'Whoa!' said Jack. 'I had that done when I was born and I couldn't walk for a year!'

Shortly after going to bed, a little girl called out: 'Daddy, Daddy, please can I have another glass of water?'

'But that's the tenth one I've given you tonight,' said the father.

'I know,' said the little girl, 'but the baby's bedroom is still on fire.'

A woman was trying to get the ketchup to come out of the bottle. During her struggle the phone rang so she asked her four-year-old daughter to answer it.

'Mum, it's the vicar,' said the little girl.

'Tell him I won't be a moment,' called out the mother.

So the little girl said: 'Mummy can't come to the phone right now. She's hitting the bottle.'

A four-year-old boy was asked to say grace before Christmas dinner. He began his prayer by thanking his family – his mother, his father, his sister, his uncle, his aunt, his grandpa and his grandma, even his dog – and then he thanked God for the food. He thanked God for the turkey, the sausage, the potatoes, the cranberry sauce, the fruit salad, the pies and the cakes. Then he paused. Everyone waited. Eventually he looked up at his mother and said: 'If I thank God for the broccoli, won't he know I'm lying?'

When Dad came home he was astonished to see his six-year-old son Alex sitting on the family dog, writing something.

'What on earth are you doing there?' he asked his son.

'Well,' Alex replied, 'the teacher told us to write an essay on our favourite animal. That's why I'm here and that's why Susie's sitting in the goldfish bowl.'

A young boy was practising spelling with magnetic letters on the refrigerator: 'cat', 'dog', 'dad' and 'mum' had been proudly displayed for all to see.

One morning while getting ready for the day, he bounded into the living room with his arms outstretched. In his hands were three magnetic letters: G-O-D.

'Look what I spelled, Mum!' he said, with a proud smile on his face.

'That's wonderful!' his mother praised him. 'Now

go and put them on the fridge so Dad can see when he gets home tonight.'

The mother happily thought that her son's Catholic education was finally having an impact. Just then, a little voice called from the kitchen: 'Mum? How do you spell "zilla"?'

Tommy came thundering down the stairs, much to his father's annoyance.

'Tommy,' he called, 'how many more times have I got to tell you to come down the stairs quietly? Now, go back up and come down like a civilized human being.'

There was a silence, and Tommy reappeared in the front room.

'That's better,' said his father. 'Now will you always come down stairs like that?'

'Suits me,' said Tommy, 'I slid down the banister!'

One day a little girl was sitting and watching her mother do the dishes at the kitchen sink. She suddenly noticed that her mother had several strands of white hair sticking out in contrast on her brunette head. She looked at her mother and asked:

'Why are some of your hairs white, Mum?'

Her mother replied teasingly: 'Well, darling, every time that you do something wrong and make me cry or unhappy, one of my hairs turns white.'

The little girl thought about this revelation for a while and then said: 'Mum, is that why all of Grandma's hairs are white?'

One day Joe's mother turned to his father and said: 'It's such a nice day, I think I'll take Joe to the zoo.'

'I wouldn't bother,' said his father. 'If they want him, let them come and get him.'

'Is your mother home?' a salesman asked a small boy.

'Yeah, she's home,' the boy said, scooting over to let him past.

The salesman rang the doorbell, got no response, knocked once, then again. Still no one came to the door.

Turning to the boy, the salesman said: 'I thought you said your mother was home?'

The kid replied: 'She is; but this isn't where I live.'

There was a little boy named Johnny who used to hang out at the local corner shop. The owner didn't know what Johnny's problem was but the boys would constantly tease him. They would always comment that he was two bricks shy of a load, or two pickles short of a barrel. To prove it, sometimes they would offer Johnny his choice between a ten-pence piece and a twenty-pence piece, and Johnny would always take the ten pence – they said, because it was bigger.

One day after Johnny grabbed the ten pence, the store owner took him aside and said: 'Johnny, those boys are making fun of you. They think you don't know the twenty pence is worth more than the ten pence. Are you grabbing the ten pence because it's bigger, or what?'

Slowly, Johnny turned towards the shop owner and said with a smile: 'Well, if I took the twenty pence, they'd stop doing it and so far I've saved twenty quid.'

A man observed a woman in the grocery store with a three-year-old girl in her trolley. As they passed the biscuit section, the child asked for cookies, and her mother told her 'no'.

The little girl immediately began to whine and

fuss, and the mother said quietly: 'Now, Laura, we just have half of the aisles left to go through; don't be upset. It won't be long.'

He passed the mother again in the cake aisle. Of course, the little girl began to shout for cakes. When she was told she couldn't have any, she began to cry.

The mother said: 'There, there, Laura, don't cry. Only two more aisles to go, and then we'll be checking out.'

The man happened to be behind the pair in the checkout queue, where the little girl began to clamour for sweets and burst into a terrible tantrum upon discovering her mother wouldn't buy any for her.

'Laura, we'll be through this checkout in five minutes, and then you can go home and have a nice nap,' the mother said.

The man followed them out to the parking lot and stopped the woman to compliment her. 'I couldn't help noticing how patient you were with little Laura,' he said.

The mother replied: 'My little girl's name is Chelsey. I'm Laura.'

A father was in church with three of his young children, including his five-year-old daughter. As was customary, he sat in the very front row so that the children could properly witness the service.

During this particular service, the minister was performing the baptism of a tiny infant. The little girl was taken by this, observing that he was saying something and pouring water over the infant's head. With a quizzical look on her face, she turned to her father and asked: 'Daddy, why is he brainwashing that baby?'

Before going to live with his father, Peter was packing everything in his room and putting it in his little red wagon. He was walking to his father's house with his wagon behind him, when he reached a steep hill. He started up the hill past the church but was constantly swearing: 'This goddamn thing is so heavy!'

A priest heard him and came out of the church. 'You shouldn't be swearing,' said the priest. 'God hears you ... He is everywhere ... He's in the church ... He's on the street ... He's everywhere.'

'Oh,' said Peter, 'is he in my wagon?'

The priest replied: 'Yes, Peter, God is in your wagon.'

Peter said: 'Well tell him to get the hell out and start pulling.'

One night, little Jack went to sleep and dreamed his Uncle Bill died.

He woke up and that evening, his dad got a call saying that Uncle Bill had died.

The next night, Jack went to sleep and dreamed his Aunt Joy died. He woke up and then that evening, his dad got a call saying that Aunt Joy had died.

He told his dad: 'Two days ago, I had a dream Uncle Bill died, and then yesterday, I had a dream Aunt Joy died.'

His dad said: 'That's just a coincidence.'

The next morning Jack told his parents: 'Last night I had a dream that my dad died.'

His dad was terrified. He had the worst day at work and took every precaution. He didn't eat any of his food in case of food poisoning, and he drove slowly in case of a car crash. When he finally got home, Jack's mother asked him how his day at work was.

'Much worse than your day, I'm sure,' his dad replied.

'I don't know,' said Jack's mother. 'The milkman dropped dead on the front porch today!'

Ben wanted to go to the zoo and pestered his parents for days. Finally his mother talked his reluctant father into taking him.

'So how was it?' his mother asked when they returned home.

'Great,' Ben replied.

'Did you and Daddy have a good time?' she asked.

'Yeah, Daddy really liked it, too,' exclaimed Ben. 'Especially when one of the animals came home at twenty to one!'

Little Sammy's mother looked out the window and noticed him 'playing church' with their three kittens. He had the kittens sitting in a row and he was preaching to them. She smiled and went about her work.

A while later she heard loud meowing and hissing and ran back to the open window to see Sammy baptizing the kittens in a tub of water.

She called out: 'Sammy, stop that! Those kittens are afraid of water!'

Johnny looked at her and said: 'They should have thought about that before they joined my church.'

A father figured that at age seven it was inevitable for his son to begin having doubts about Santa Claus. Sure enough, one day his son came home from school and said: 'Dad, I know something about Santa Claus, the Easter Bunny and the Tooth Fairy.'

Taking a deep breath, his father asked him: 'What is that?'

The young boy replied: 'They're all nocturnal.'

Katie was a typical four-year-old girl – cute, inquisitive and bright.

When she expressed difficulty in grasping the concept of marriage, her father decided to pull out his wedding photo album, thinking visual images would help. On one page after another, he pointed out the bride arriving at the church, the entrance, the wedding ceremony, the recessional and the reception.

'Now do you understand?' he asked his daughter.

'I think so,' she replied. 'That was when Mummy came to work for us?'

The father of five children had won a toy at a raffle. He called his kids together to ask which one should have the present.

'Who is the most obedient?' he asked. 'Who never talks back to Mother? Who does everything she says?'

Five small voices answered in unison: 'Okay, Dad, you get the toy.'

Little Timmy was in the garden filling in a hole when his neighbour peered over the fence. Interested in what the cheeky-faced youngster was up to, he politely asked: 'What are you doing, Tim?'

'My hamster died,' replied the boy tearfully, without looking up. 'I've just buried him.'

The neighbour was concerned. 'That's an awfully big hole for a hamster, isn't it?' he asked.

Tim patted down the last heap of earth, then replied: 'That's because he's inside your cat!'

Two young country brothers were knocking around one lazy summer day and thought it would be a good prank to push over the outhouse. They crept up like a couple of commandos, pushed the outhouse over on one side and headed for the woods. They circled round and returned home an hour later from a completely different direction, trying to divert suspicion from themselves.

On their return, their father approached them and bellowed: 'Did you two push the outhouse over this afternoon?'

The older boy replied: 'As learned in school, I cannot tell a lie. Yes, Dad, we pushed over the outhouse this afternoon.'

Hearing this, the father flew into a rage and sent them to bed without supper.

In the morning, the two boys meekly approached the breakfast table and took their seats. Everything was quiet until their father finally asked: 'Have you two learned your lesson?'

'Sure, Dad,' said the younger brother, 'but in school we learned that George Washington admitted to his father that he'd chopped down a cherry tree and he was forgiven because he told the truth.'

'Yes,' said the father, 'but George's dad wasn't in the cherry tree when he chopped it down!'

A wife invited some people to dinner. At the table, she turned to her six-year-old daughter and asked: 'Would you like to say grace?'

'I wouldn't know what to say,' the girl replied.

'Just say what you hear Mummy say,' her father answered.

The daughter bowed her head and said: 'Lord, why on earth did I invite all these people to dinner?'

A teenager wanted to earn some money so he decided to offer his services as a handyman and started canvassing a wealthy neighbourhood. He went to the front door of the first house and asked the owner if he had any jobs for him to do. 'Well, you can paint my porch,' said the house owner. 'How much will you charge?'

The boy said: 'How about fifty pounds?'

The man agreed and told him that the paint and ladders were in the garage.

The man's wife, who was inside the house, heard the conversation and said to her husband: 'Does that boy realize that the porch goes all the way around the house?'

The man replied: 'He should. He was standing on it. Anyway that's his problem.'

A short time later, the teenager came to the door to collect his money.

'You're finished already?' asked the man in surprise.

'Yes,' the teenager answered, 'and I had paint left over, so I gave it two coats.'

Impressed by the teenager's quick work, the man reached in his pocket for the fifty pounds.

'And by the way,' the boy added, 'that's not a Porch, it's a Ferrari.'

A farmer was driving along the road with a load of fertilizer. A little boy, playing in front of his house, saw him and called out: 'What have you got in your truck?'

'Fertilizer,' the farmer replied.

'What are you going to do with it?' asked the little boy.

'Put it on strawberries,' answered the farmer.

'You ought to live with us,' the little boy advised him. 'We put sugar and cream on ours.'

Death

As an old man lay dying in his bedroom, his family sat in the lounge and debated his funeral arrangements.

Son Jonathan said: 'We'll give him a great send-off, with a band, a fleet of limos and hundreds of guests.'

Daughter Jane disagreed. 'Why waste all that money on a lavish funeral? He's not going to be there to appreciate it. We'll just have family and a few close friends. One car is all we'll need.'

Grandson Ben suggested: 'He's always loved flowers, so we should get dozens of bouquets of his favourite roses.'

Granddaughter Lucy countered: 'That's a total waste of money. One small bouquet will be quite sufficient.'

Eventually the rest of the family agreed that it would be pointless to spend a lot of money on the funeral. Instead they resolved to keep costs down to a minimum.

Just then the old man's voice could be heard from the bedroom. 'Why don't you get me my shoes?' he groaned. 'I'll walk to the cemetery!'

An elderly newcomer to town asked his neighbour: 'What's the death rate around here?'

'Same as everywhere,' replied the neighbour. 'One per person.'

On vacation in the Bahamas, a wealthy English businessman received a telegram from his butler, which read simply: 'Cat dead.' Upset at the loss of his pet, the businessman flew straight home and gave the cat a proper burial. Afterwards he chided the butler for the callous nature of the telegram.

'You should break bad news gently,' he said. 'If I had been telling you that your cat had died, I would have sent a telegram saying: "The cat is on the roof and can't get down." Then a couple of hours later I would have sent you another telegram saying: "The cat has fallen off the roof and is badly hurt." Finally a couple of hours after that, I would have sent you a third telegram saying: "The cat has sadly passed away." In that way, you would have been gradually prepared for the bad news and would have been able to cope with it better.'

'I understand, sir,' said the butler. 'I shall bear that in mind in future.'

The businessman flew back to resume his vacation in the Bahamas but three days later he received another telegram from his butler. It read: 'Your mother is on the roof and can't get down.'

Why do cemeteries have fences around them?
—Because people are dying to get in.

A young man met his friend in a bar and said: 'My grandmother died last week – on her ninety-fourth birthday.'

'Oh, that's sad,' said the friend.

'Yes. We were only halfway through giving her the bumps at the time.'

Taking flowers to a cemetery, a woman noticed an old Chinese man placing a bowl of rice on a grave.

Puzzled by the choice of memorial, she said to him: 'When exactly do you expect your friend to come up and eat the rice?'

The Chinese man smiled: 'The same time your friend comes up to smell the flowers.'

When Michael was a young minister, a funeral director asked him to hold a grave side service for a homeless man with no family or friends. The funeral was to be at a cemetery way out in the country. It was a new cemetery and this man was the first to be laid to rest there.

Michael was not familiar with the area and became lost. He didn't ask for directions but finally found the cemetery about an hour late. He saw a mechanical digger there and a crew of men eating their lunch. The hearse was nowhere to be seen.

Michael apologized to the men for being late. As he looked into the open grave, he saw the vault lid already in place. He told the men that he would not keep them long but that this was the proper thing to do. The men, still eating their lunch, gathered around the opening.

Michael was young and enthusiastic and poured

out his heart and soul as he preached. The men joined in with Praise the Lord, Amen and Glory! He got so into the service that he preached for nearly an hour.

When the service was finally over, Michael said a prayer and walked to his car. As he opened the door, he heard one of the men say: 'I never saw anything like that before and I've been putting in septic systems for twenty years!'

When her late husband's will was read out, a widow discovered that he had left most of his money to another woman. Understandably bitter, she tried to have the inscription on his tombstone changed but the mason told her: 'Sorry, I have already inscribed "Rest in Peace" as you asked. It's too late to change it.'

'Very well,' she said icily. 'Just add, "Until We Meet Again".'

Two elderly spinsters were sitting in the lounge of their retirement home. One said to the other: 'Did you hear that Ethel has just cremated her fourth husband?'

'Well,' sighed the other, 'that's how it is. Some of us can't find a husband, and others have husbands to burn!'

Bill, Dan and Lou were working on a building site when Bill tripped on the scaffolding and fell to his death. Dan was sent to break the news to Bill's wife but he returned to the site an hour later carrying a six-pack.

'Where did you get the beer?' asked Lou.

'Bill's wife gave it to me,' said Dan.

'What?!' exclaimed Lou. 'You told the woman that her husband was dead and she gave you beer?!'

'It wasn't quite like that,' said Dan. 'When she answered the door, I said to her: "You must be Bill's widow." She said: "I'm not a widow." And I said: "Want to bet me a six-pack?"'

When Ted's wife died, he was so distraught that he collapsed sobbing at her funeral. A friend tried to comfort him. 'Listen, Ted, I know it's tough for you right now but time really is a great healer. You never know, in six or seven months you might even find yourself a new woman.'

'Six or seven months?' wailed Ted. 'What am I going to do tonight?'

After suffering a miserable marriage for thirty-four years, a husband shed few tears when his wife died. Rather than spend money on her funeral, he arranged for her to be buried on the cheap in their back garden.

A week later, a friend of the deceased called round to pay her respects. Seeing the wife's bottom sticking up out of the ground, she asked: 'Did you bury her like that as an expression of your love and devotion – so that there would always be something visible to remind you of her?'

'Certainly not,' said the husband. 'It's somewhere to park my bike!'

A new young church minister had a passion for animal rights, so he was appalled to see one of the female members of his congregation walking down the street in a long fur coat. Marching over to her, he demanded: 'What poor creature had to die so that you could wear that coat?'

The startled woman replied: 'My aunt.'

Dentists

A husband and wife visited the dentist. The man explained to the dentist that he wanted a tooth extracted. 'I don't want gas or Novocain because I'm in a terrible hurry. Just extract the tooth as quickly as possible.'

'You're a brave man,' said the dentist. 'Now show me which tooth it is.'

The husband turned to his wife and said: 'Open your mouth wide, dear, and show the dentist which tooth it is.'

A boy arrived from home school and said: 'Mum, I thought you said my trip to the school dentist would be painless.'

'Did he hurt you, dear?' asked the concerned mother.

'No,' said the boy, 'but he screamed when I bit his finger.'

A Texan went to the dentist.

'Your teeth look fine,' said the dentist. 'You don't need anything doing.'

'Drill anyway,' said the Texan. 'I feel lucky.'

'Open wider,' said the dentist as he began examining the patient. 'Goodness!' he exclaimed. 'You've got the biggest cavity I've ever seen, the biggest cavity I've ever seen.'

'Okay, Doc,' replied the patient. 'I'm scared enough without you saying it twice!'

'I didn't,' said the dentist. 'That was the echo!'

While treating a patient, the dentist suddenly begged: 'Please can you do me a favour?'

'I'll try,' replied the puzzled patient.

'Could you give out a few of your loudest, most painful screams?' asked the dentist.

'But what you're doing isn't at all painful,' said the patient.

'I know,' said the dentist. 'But I've got a waiting room full of patients and I don't want to miss the match, which kicks off at three!'

A patient asked his dentist: 'How much to get my teeth straightened?'

'Fifteen thousand pounds,' replied the dentist.

The patient headed straight for the door.

'Where are you going?' asked the dentist.

'To a plastic surgeon to get my mouth bent!'

What does the dentist of the year get?
—A little plaque.

A man felt nervous about making an appointment with the dentist but finally he plucked up courage and phoned the surgery.

'I'm sorry,' said the receptionist, 'but the dentist is out at the moment.'

'Thank you,' said the man, relieved. 'When will he be out again?'

Patient: How much to have this tooth pulled?
Dentist: Seventy pounds.
Patient: Seventy pounds just for a few minutes work?
Dentist: Well, I can extract it really slowly if you like.

Patient: Can you recommend anything for yellow teeth?
Dentist: A brown tie!

Patient: What should I do with all the gold and silver in my mouth?
Dentist: Don't smile in a bad neighbourhood.

Doctors and Nurses

A newly hired nurse was startled when a surgeon doing his rounds went through the wards shouting: 'Tetanus! Typhoid! Measles!'

'Why does he keep doing that?' the nurse asked a colleague.

'Oh, he just likes calling the shots around here.'

A man was in hospital and became increasingly irritated by the patronizing attitude of one of the nurses. Every morning she would tuck in his sheets, pat him on the head and ask: 'And how are we today?'

He decided to take revenge at breakfast the next day. Having been given a urine bottle to fill, he instead emptied his apple juice into the container. When the nurse came to examine the supposed sample, she remarked: 'We appear to be a little cloudy today.'

To her horror the man snatched the urine bottle from her, drank the contents and replied sarcastically: 'Well, I'll run it through the system again and see if I can filter it better this time!'

'Doctor, Doctor, please help me. Some mornings I wake up and think I'm Mickey Mouse. Other days I think I'm Donald Duck.'

'Hmmmm. Tell me, how long have you been having these disney spells?'

Patient: Doctor, are you sure I'm suffering from glandular fever? I heard once about a doctor treating a patient for glandular fever but he ended dying from typhoid.

Doctor: Don't worry; you won't have that problem with me. If I treat a patient for glandular fever, they'll die of glandular fever.

'Doctor, Doctor, I can't pronounce my Fs, Ts or Hs.'
   'You can't say fairer than that!'

Scalpel ... sutures ... clamp ... oops ... pen ... death certificate!'

'Doctor, Doctor, I think I'm shrinking.'
   'Don't worry, you'll just have to be a little patient.'

'Doctor, Doctor, my wife thinks she's an elevator.'
   'Please tell her to come in.'
   'She can't, she doesn't stop at this floor.'

After losing his ear in a car crash, a man was given a pig's ear. Two months after the transplant he returned to hospital for a check-up.

   'Everything looks fine,' said the surgeon. 'Any problems with your hearing?'

   'Not really,' replied the man, 'although I do get a bit of crackling!'

A doctor told his patient: 'I have some good news and some bad news.'

The worried patient said: 'I'll have the good news first.'

The doctor said: 'They're going to name a disease after you!'

A man went to the doctor because he was feeling run down. The doctor examined him but could find nothing wrong.

'Do you smoke?' asked the doctor.

'No.'

'Do you drink to excess?'

'No.'

'What about your diet? What do you eat on an average day?'

'Snooker balls,' replied the patient. 'I have two reds for breakfast, three yellows for lunch and four blues and a brown for dinner.'

'Well, that explains it,' said the doctor. 'You're not eating enough greens!'

'Doctor, Doctor, I think I swallowed a pillow.'
   'How do you feel?'
   'A little down in the mouth.'

Suffering from a really bad dose of 'flu, an outraged patient yelled at the doctor's receptionist: 'Three lousy weeks before I can see a doctor? I could be dead by then!'

   'In that event,' said the receptionist sternly, 'could you please get your wife to call the surgery and cancel the appointment?'

In the course of his ward rounds a hospital consultant pointed out an X-ray to a group of medical students. 'As you can see,' he said, 'the patient limps because her left fibula and tibia are radically arched. John, what would you do in a case like this?'

   'Well,' pondered the medical student. 'I suppose I would limp too!'

Patient: I have spent eighty per cent of my life savings on doctors.
Doctor: Why didn't you come to me earlier?

Two women were standing at the bus stop discussing their recent illnesses.

One said: 'My doctor promised he would have me on my feet within two weeks.'

'And did he?' asked the other.

'Yes, I had to sell my car to pay his bill!'

A fifty-year-old farmhand was being treated in hospital for a broken leg. 'How did it happen?' asked the doctor.

'Well, Doc,' began the farmhand, 'thirty years ago ...'

'I'm not interested in your life story,' said the doctor brusquely. 'I want to know how you came to break your leg this morning.'

'As I was saying,' continued the farmhand. 'Thirty years ago when I first started working on the farm, one night, just as I was getting ready for bed, the farmer's beautiful daughter knocked on the door of my room and asked me whether there was anything I wanted. I said: "No, thanks, everything is fine."

'"Are you sure?" she asked.

'"I'm sure," I said.

'"Isn't there anything at all I can do for you?" she said.

'"No, I don't think so," I replied.'

'Look, I don't mean to be rude,' the doctor interrupted, 'but I'm a very busy man and I don't see what this story from thirty years ago has to do with your broken leg.'

'Well, this morning,' the farmhand explained, 'when it finally dawned on me what she meant, I fell off the roof!'

A woman visited her doctor because she had a very heavy cold. The doctor prescribed some tablets but they didn't work. On her next visit the doctor gave her an injection but that didn't work either. On her third visit the doctor suggested she go home, take a hot bath, then open all the windows and stand in the draught.

'But I'll catch pneumonia,' said the patient.

'I know,' said the doctor, 'but I can cure pneumonia.'

A young man went to the doctor covered in cuts and bruises. The doctor was shocked when he saw them and asked: 'How on earth did you get these?'

'Well,' said the young man, 'I was walking along the street, minding my own business, when a huge beetle attacked me for about ten minutes.'

'I know,' said the doctor, 'there's a nasty bug going around.'

A man went to his doctor for a routine medical examination. The doctor asked him how much he weighed.

'About twelve stone,' the man answered.

'Please step on the scales,' said the doctor. 'Hmmm, fifteen stone seven pounds. And your height?'

'Six foot,' replied the man.

The doctor measured him. 'Five foot seven inches. Now, I'd like to take your blood pressure. Please roll up your sleeve.'

The man rolled up his sleeve. 'Well,' said the doctor, 'that's very high.'

'Of course it's high!' exclaimed the man. 'I came in here tall and slim and now I'm short and fat!'

A man visited his doctor and said that he was considering having a vasectomy.

'That's a really big decision,' said the doctor. 'You must go home and discuss it with your family.'

'I already have,' said the man. 'They're in favour, twelve to one!'

A doctor was driving his four-year-old daughter to nursery when she started playing with the stethoscope he had accidentally left on the back seat. He glanced into his mirror and smiled at the thought that perhaps his daughter would follow in his footsteps.

Then the child spoke into the instrument: 'Welcome to McDonald's. May I take your order?'

While his wife was out shopping for the day, a husband took the opportunity to paint the toilet seat. But on her return, he forgot to warn her about the wet paint and when she sat on the toilet seat it became stuck to her behind.

Unable to remove the seat from her backside, the husband wrapped her in a big coat to conceal her embarrassment and drove her to the doctor.

In the doctor's office the husband lifted his wife's coat to reveal the problem. 'Doctor,' he asked, 'have you ever seen anything like this before?'

'Well, yes,' replied the doctor, 'but not framed like that.'

A patient was sitting in the waiting room of a world-renowned specialist. When she was summoned to see the great man, he asked: 'Who did you see before coming to me?'

'My family doctor,' replied the patient.

'Your family doctor!' scoffed the specialist. 'What a waste of time! Tell me what sort of useless advice did he give you?'

'He recommended I come to you!'

A respected hospital consultant had just returned home from work and was relaxing on the sofa when the phone rang. He answered the call and at the other end of the line was the familiar voice of a colleague.

'We need a fourth player for poker,' said the colleague.

'I'll be right over,' whispered the consultant.

As he was putting on his coat, his wife asked: 'Is it serious?'

'Yes, quite serious,' he replied gravely. 'In fact there are three doctors there already.'

Old Doctor Evans called at the home of a woman patient. He asked the woman's husband if he could get him a hammer from his tool shed. So the man fetched the doctor a hammer. Then the doctor asked the man if he could get him a hacksaw, some pliers and a screwdriver.

'What are you going to do to my wife?' asked the alarmed husband.

'Nothing until I can get my bag open,' replied the doctor.

'Doctor,' shouted the woman, as she barged her way into his room. 'I want you to tell me frankly what is wrong with me.'

He surveyed the woman for a few moments then said: 'Madam, I have just three things to tell you. First, you need to lose at least twenty pounds. Second, you should use about half as much lipstick and rouge. And third, I'm the chartered accountant – the doctor is on the next floor!'

'Doctor, I seem to have lost my memory,' said the patient. 'I can't remember anything anymore. I can't remember my house number. I can't remember the names of my kids. I can't remember the make of car I drive. I can't even remember how I got here.'

'How long have you been like this?' asked the doctor.

'Been like what?'

What Doctors Say and What They Really Mean:

This should be taken care of right away.
Translation: I'd planned a trip to Florida next month but this is so easy and profitable that I want to fix it before it cures itself.

Let me schedule you for some tests.
Translation: I have a forty-five per cent interest in the lab.

If it doesn't clear up in a week, give me a call.
Translation: With any luck, whatever it is, it will clear up by itself.

This may hurt a little.
Translation: Last week two patients bit through their tongues.

Let's see how it develops.
Translation: With time, hopefully it will turn into something that can be cured.

I'd like to prescribe a new drug.
Translation: I'm writing a paper and would like to use you as a guinea pig.

If the symptoms persist, call for an appointment.
Translation: I'm going on vacation for a month.

A newly qualified young doctor moved into a rural community to replace a retiring medic. The older man suggested that the young doctor accompany him on his final round of house calls so that the villagers could get to know him. At the first house they visited, the younger doctor listened while the older doctor and an elderly lady discussed the weather, their grandchildren and the forthcoming harvest festival. After a while the older doctor asked the patient what the problem was.

'I've been feeling really sick, Doctor,' she replied.

'I think you have been eating too much fruit. Why don't you cut back on the amount of fresh fruit you eat and see if that helps?' he advised.

As they left the house the young doctor asked his more senior colleague how he reached his diagnosis so quickly and without even examining her.

'I didn't feel it necessary to examine her,' he explained. 'Did you notice that I dropped my stethoscope while I was in there? Well, when I bent down to pick it up I noticed half a dozen banana peels in the waste bin. That was what was probably making her ill.'

The young doctor was impressed by his colleague's detective work and asked whether he could try the same principle at the next house. Their next call was an elderly widow. They spent a few minutes discussing the weather, the grandchildren and the forthcoming harvest festival before the young doctor asked her what the problem was.

'I've been feeling tired and run-down lately,' the patent explained. 'I just don't have the energy I used to.'

'You've probably been doing too much work for the church,' suggested the young doctor without examining her. 'Maybe you should ease up a bit and see if that helps.'

After they left, the senior doctor said: 'Your

diagnosis is probably correct but do you mind explaining how you came to that conclusion?'

'Sure,' replied his young colleague. 'Just like you I dropped my stethoscope on the floor. When I bent down to pick it up, I looked up and saw the vicar hiding under the bed!'

His arm covered in sores, a man decided to go to the doctor.

'What is your job?' asked the doctor.

'I work in a circus,' replied the man. 'I give enemas to the elephants. I have to ram my right arm up their backsides and clean them out.'

'Heavens!' exclaimed the doctor. 'No wonder your arm's in such a state! Have you ever considered looking for another job?'

'What?' said the man. 'And give up show business?'

On his first visit to his attractive new woman doctor, a man was given a thorough check-up.

'Right,' she said, 'I'm going to put my hand on your back and I want you to say eighty-eight.'

He felt her soft, cool hand on his back and said, 'Eighty-eight.'

'Now I'm going to put my hand on your neck, and again I want you to say eighty-eight.'

He felt her smooth hand on his neck and said, 'Eighty-eight.'

'Now, I'm going to put my hand on your chest, and again could you please say eighty-eight?'

Feeling her gentle hand on his chest, he said: 'One, two, three, four ...'

A woman called the hospital to inquire after a patient's health. 'I'd like to know if Miriam Ratzenberg in room 314 is getting better.'

'Yes, Mrs Ratzenberg is doing very well,' said the ward sister. 'She's had two full meals, her temperature and blood pressure is fine, she may be taken off the heart monitor later today and if she continues improving, Dr Cohen is going to send her home on Tuesday.'

'Thank God!' said the caller. 'That's wonderful news!'

'From your reaction, I take it you must be a relative or a very close friend?' said the nurse.

'Actually,' replied the caller, 'I'm Miriam Ratzenberg. Dr Cohen never tells me anything!'

Two surgeons were enjoying a drink at their private club. One said: 'I operated on your next-door neighbour last week.'

'What for?' asked the other.

'About forty thousand pounds.'

'What did he have?'

'Oh, about forty thousand pounds.'

One wet and miserable day two children were deciding what indoor game they could play.

One said: 'I know, let's play doctor.'

'Good idea,' said the other. 'You operate and I'll sue!'

A prisoner visited the prison doctor and said: 'Look here, Doctor, you've already removed my spleen, tonsils, adenoids and one of my kidneys. I only came to see if you could get me out of this place!'

The doctor replied: 'I am, bit by bit.'

A Brief History of Medicine

'Doctor, I have an ear ache.'

2000 BC – 'Here, eat this root.'

1000 BC – 'That root is heathen, say this prayer.'

1800 AD – 'That prayer is superstition, drink this potion.'

1940 AD – 'That potion is snake oil, swallow this pill.'

1985 AD – 'That pill is ineffective, take this antibiotic.'

2010 AD – 'That antibiotic is artificial. Here, eat this root.'

At a party a woman was talking to a doctor. 'What kind of doctor are you?' she asked.

'I'm a naval surgeon,' the doctor replied.

'My!' she exclaimed. 'How you doctors specialize!'

A woman went to a doctor and asked: 'Please, Doctor, can you help me? I get so nervous and frightened during driving tests.'

'Don't worry,' said the doctor, 'you'll pass eventually.'

'But, I'm the examiner,' replied the woman.

A man walked into a doctor's surgery and the receptionist asked what he had.

'Shingles,' he replied.

So she took down his name, address and date of birth, and told him to take a seat.

A few minutes later, a nursing assistant came out and asked him what he had.

'Shingles,' he answered.

So she made a note of his weight, height and complete medical history, and told him to wait in the examining room.

Ten minutes later, a nurse came in and asked him what he had.

'Shingles,' he said.

So she gave him a blood test, a blood pressure test and an electrocardiogram, and told him to remove all of his clothes and wait for the doctor.

Fifteen minutes later the doctor came in and asked him what he had.

'Shingles,' he replied.

'Where?' asked the doctor.

'Outside in the truck. Where do you want them?'

Three doctors – a general practitioner, a pathologist and a surgeon – were out on a duck shoot. Suddenly a bird flew overhead. The general practitioner stared at it and said: 'Looks like a duck, flies like a duck … it's probably a duck.' He then took aim but missed and the bird flew off.

When the next bird flew overhead, the pathologist looked at it before flicking through the pages of a bird book. 'Hmmm. Green wings, yellow beak, quacking sound … might be a duck.' He raised his gun to shoot it but the bird was long gone.

A third bird then flew over. The surgeon raised his gun and, almost without looking, scored a direct hit. As the bird fell to the ground, the surgeon turned to the pathologist and said: 'Go see if that was a duck.'

Patient: Doctor, I keep stealing things. Can you give me something for it?

Doctor: Try these pills. If they don't work, bring me back a DVD player.

Drunks

A man was always in trouble with his wife for arriving home drunk late at night. Every evening he would go to his favourite bar, stagger home around midnight and make such a noise as he struggled to open the front door that his wife would wake up and give him hell. Even so, he continued with his daily drinking.

One day the poor wife was complaining to her sister about his behaviour and how it was destroying their marriage. The sister suggested that instead of shouting and screaming at him when he came home drunk, she should adopt a more conciliatory approach. 'Why not try a little love and tenderness and welcome him home with a kiss? You never know, he might change his ways.' The wife promised to give it a try.

That night, the husband arrived home just after midnight in his usual drunken state. His wife heard him struggling to get the key in the door and quickly let him in. But instead of yelling at him, she gently took him by the arm, sat him down in his favourite armchair, removed his shoes and fetched his slippers. After cuddling up to him for a few minutes, she whispered: 'It's getting late, darling. I think we should go upstairs to bed now.'

The husband slurred: 'Sure, why not? I'll be in trouble anyway when I get home!'

A drunk was staggering down the street when he saw a tradesman trying to adjust the nosebag on a cart horse.

'You'll never do it!' yelled the drunk. 'You'll never do it!'

'Never do what?' asked the tradesman.

'You'll never fit that big horse into that small bag.'

A man came home from the pub at one o'clock in a drunken state and as he crept through the front door he heard his wife moving about upstairs. 'Oh, hell!' he thought. 'I don't want her to know I've been drinking all evening. I know, I'll pretend I've been reading downstairs for the last couple of hours.'

So he went into the living-room and sat down. A few minutes later, his wife came downstairs and poked her head around the door.

'What are you doing?' she asked.

'Reading, dear,' he replied, trying to sound sober. 'Just reading.'

'Shut up, you drunken idiot,' she said. 'Now close that suitcase and come to bed.'

A drunk was proudly showing off his new apartment to a couple of friends late one night. He led the way to his bedroom where there was a big brass gong and a mallet.

'What's with that big brass gong?' one of the guests asked.

'It's not a gong. It's a talking clock,' the drunk replied.

'A talking clock?' asked his astonished friend. 'Seriously?'

'Yeah,' replied the drunk.

'How does it work?' asked the friend, squinting at it.

'Watch,' said the drunk. He then picked up the mallet, gave the gong an ear-shattering pound and stepped back.

The three stood looking at one another for a moment. Suddenly, someone on the other side of the wall screamed: 'What are you doing? It's three-fifteen in the morning!'

After drinking freely at a lavish company party in New York, two English business executives staggered out into the street. Max crossed the street while Kevin stumbled down into the subway. When Max reached the other side, he spotted Kevin emerging from the subway stairs.

'Where have you been?' demanded Max.

'I dunno,' said Kevin, much the worse for wear, 'but you should see the train set that guy has in his basement.'

Things that are difficult to say when you're drunk:

* Innovative
* Preliminary
* Proliferation
* Archaeological

Things that are very difficult to say when you're drunk:

* Specificity
* British Constitution
* Passive-aggressive disorder
* Transubstantiation

Things that are absolutely impossible to say when you're drunk:

* Thanks, but I don't want to sleep with you.
* Nope, no more booze for me.
* Sorry, but you're not really my type.
* No kebab for me, thank you.
* No, I'll look silly in false breasts.
* I'm not interested in fighting you.
* Oh, I just couldn't – no one wants to hear me sing.
* No way, that looks far too dangerous.
* Of course, Officer. You're only doing your job.
* Thank you, but I won't make any attempt to dance
* I must be going home now as I have work in the morning.

A man walked into a bar in Dublin, ordered three pints of Guinness and sat in the back of the room, drinking a sip out of each one in turn. When he finished them, he went back to the bar and ordered three more.

The bartender said to him: 'You know, a pint goes flat after I draw it; it would taste better if you bought one at a time.'

The man replied: 'Well, you see, I have two brothers. One is in America, the other is in Australia and I'm here in Dublin. When we all left home, we promised that we'd drink this way to remember the days when we drank together.'

The bartender admitted that this was a nice custom and let the man continue drinking.

The man became a regular in the bar and always drank the same way, ordering three pints and drinking them in turn. Then one day, he came in and only ordered two pints. All the other regulars noticed and fell silent. When he went back to the bar for the second round, the bartender said to him quietly: 'I don't want to intrude on your grief but I wanted to offer my condolences on your great loss.'

The man looked confused for a moment, then a light dawned in his eye and he laughed. 'Oh, no,' he said, 'everyone's fine. I've just quit drinking.'

A drunk was stumbling down an alley carrying a box with holes in the side. He bumped into a friend who asked: 'What do you have in there, pal?'

'It's a mongoose,' the drunk answered.

'What have you got that for?'

'Well, you know how drunk I can get? When I get drunk I see snakes and I'm scared to death of snakes. That's why I got this mongoose, for protection.'

'You idiot!' his friend said. 'Those are imaginary snakes!'

'That's okay,' said the drunk, showing his friend the interior of the box. 'So is the mongoose.'

A Good Samaritan was walking home late one night when he came upon this drunk on the pavement outside a block of apartments. Wanting to help, he asked the drunk: 'Do you live here?'

The drunk confirmed that he did.

'Would you like me to help you upstairs?' the Samaritan asked.

The drunk confirmed that he would.

When they got up to the second floor, the Samaritan asked: 'Which floor do you live on?'

'This one,' the drunk answered.

Then the Samaritan got to thinking that maybe

he didn't want to face the man's irate and tired wife in case she thought he was the one who had got her husband drunk. So he opened the first door he came to and shoved him through it before going back downstairs. However, when he went back outside, there was another drunk.

So he asked that drunk: 'Do you live here?'

The drunk confirmed that he did.

'Would you like me to help you upstairs?' the Samaritan asked.

The drunk confirmed that he would.

When they got up to the second floor, the Samaritan asked: 'Which floor do you live on?'

'This one,' the drunk answered.

Again deciding that he didn't want to face the drunk's wife, he put him in the same door with the first drunk. Then he went back downstairs and outside where he was surprised to find another drunk. So the Samaritan approached him but before he could strike up a conversation, the drunk staggered over to a policeman and cried: 'Please, Officer, protect me from this man. He's been doing nothing all night long but taking me upstairs and throwing me down the elevator shaft!'

A drunk staggered into a library, went up to the counter and ordered a double Scotch. The librarian attempted to explain what the building was but the drunk was too far gone to understand.

'I want a double Scotch,' he repeated, slurring his words.

'Listen,' said the librarian, exasperated, 'we do not serve Scotch here. Do you understand?'

'Okay, pal, no problem. I understand,' said the drunk. 'Give me a beer.'

A new guy in town walked into a bar and read a sign that hung over the bar: Free beer for the person who can pass our test!

So the man asked the barman what the test was.

The barman replied: 'Well, first you have to drink that whole gallon of pepper tequila, the whole thing at once and you can't make a face while doing it. Second, there's an alligator out back with a sore tooth. You have to remove it with your bare hands. Third, there's a woman upstairs who's never had an orgasm. You've got to make things right for her.'

The man said: 'Well, as much as I would love free beer, I won't do it. You have to be nuts to drink a gallon of pepper tequila and then get crazier from there.'

But after a few drinks, the man reconsidered and asked: 'Where's that tequila?'

He grabbed the gallon of tequila with both hands and downed it with a big slurp, tears streaming down his face.

Next, he staggered out back and soon all the people inside heard the most frightening roaring and thumping, then silence.

The man staggered back into the bar, his shirt ripped and big scratches all over his body.

'Now,' he said, 'where's that woman with the sore tooth?'

Returning to his hotel room after a few too many drinks, a drunken businessman walked into the elevator shaft and immediately plunged five floors.

Lying bloodied and bruised and flat on his back, he stared back along the shaft and yelled: 'I wanted to go up, dammit!'

A wife was in bed with her lover when she heard her husband's key in the door. 'Stay where you are,' she whispered. 'He's so drunk he won't even notice you're in bed with me.'

Sure enough, the husband lurched into bed none the wiser but, a few minutes later, through a drunken haze, he saw six feet sticking out at the end of the bed. He turned to his wife and said: 'Hey, there are six feet in this bed. There should only be four. What's going on?'

'Nonsense,' said his wife. 'You're so drunk you miscounted. Get out of bed and try again. You can see better from over there.'

The husband climbed out of bed and counted: 'One, two, three, four. You're right, you know.'

A drunk staggered into a bar and shouted: 'A double whisky please, barman, and a drink for everyone here ... and while you're at it, have one yourself.'

'Well, thank you, sir,' said the barman and he proceeded to pour everyone their drinks.

Moments later the guy shouted: 'Another whisky for me, and the same again for everyone else.'

The barman looked a little worried now and said: 'Excuse me, sir, but don't you think you should pay me for that last round first?'

The guy slurred: 'I can't. I don't have any money.'

With this the barman flew into a rage and literally threw the drunk out of the bar.

About twenty minutes later though, the guy

staggered back in and shouted out: 'A double whisky for me, and a drink for all my friends.'

'I suppose you'll be offering me a drink, too?' the barman asked, marvelling at the guy's nerve.

'Not likely,' slurred the drunk. 'You get nasty when you've had a drink!'

When a drunk rolled into a pub, the bartender refused to serve him. 'You've had too much to drink,' he told him. 'I'm not letting you have any more.'

The drunk left without a fuss but five minutes later he returned. The bartender would not budge. 'I'm not giving you any more alcohol,' he insisted. 'You've had more than enough already.'

The drunk left quietly but five minutes later the door opened and the drunk lurched in yet again. 'Listen to me,' said the bartender firmly. 'I'm not serving you. You're way too drunk.'

'I guess I must be,' said the drunk, nodding. 'The last two places said the same thing.'

A man walked into a bar and ordered a twelve-year-old Scotch. The bartender, believing that the customer would not be able to tell the difference, served him a shot of the cheap three-year-old house Scotch that had been poured into an empty bottle of the good stuff.

The man took a sip and spat the Scotch out on the bar. He glared at the barman and said: 'This is the cheapest three-year-old Scotch you can buy. I'm not paying for it. Now, give me a good twelve-year-old Scotch.'

The bartender, now feeling a bit of a challenge, poured him a much better quality, six-year-old scotch.

The man took a sip and spat it out on the bar. 'This is only six-year-old Scotch,' he complained. 'I won't pay for this and I insist on a good, twelve-year-old Scotch.'

The bartender finally relented and served the man his best quality, twelve-year-old Scotch.

An old drunk, who had witnessed the entire episode from his seat at the end of the bar, walked down to the finicky Scotch drinker. He set a glass down in front of him and asked: 'What do you think of this?'

The Scotch expert took a sip and, in disgust, violently spat out the liquid and yelled: 'Why, this tastes like pee!'

'That's right,' said the drunk. 'Now tell me how old I am!'

A drunken man went up to a woman at a party and embraced her clumsily. After she slapped him in the face, he said: 'I'm so sorry, I thought you were my wife. You look just like her.'

'Who'd want to be married to you!' she raged. 'Look at the state of you – a drunken, clumsy, lecherous brute!'

'Good heavens!' exclaimed the drunk. 'You talk like her, too!'

A woman grabbed her husband as he stumbled through the front door.

'What do you think you're doing coming home half drunk?' she yelled.

'Sorry, honey,' he replied. 'I ran out of money.'

A drunk staggered through the front door of a bar, sat himself on a stool and asked the bartender for a drink. The bartender politely informed the man that he already seemed to have had plenty to drink, and as a result he would not be serving him any more liquor but would call him a cab if he needed one.

The drunk was briefly surprised then softly scoffed, grumbled, climbed down off the bar stool and staggered out the front door.

A few minutes later, the same drunk stumbled in the side door of the bar. He wobbled up to the bar and hollered for a drink. The bartender came over and politely but firmly refused to serve him. Again, the bartender offered to call a cab for him.

The drunk looked angrily at the bartender for a moment, cursed him and showed himself out the side door, all the while grumbling and shaking his head.

A few minutes later, the same drunk burst in through the back door of the bar. He clambered on a bar stool, gathered his wits and belligerently ordered a drink. The bartender came over and emphatically reminded the man that he was clearly drunk, would be served no drinks and that either a cab or the police would be called immediately.

The surprised drunk looked at the bartender and in hopeless anguish, cried: 'Man! How many bars do you work at?'

Englishman, Irishman, Scotsman

An Englishman, an Irishman and a Scotsman were working together on a building site. At lunchtime the Englishman opened his lunch box and groaned: 'Not cheese sandwiches again! Every day it's cheese sandwiches. I swear, if I get cheese sandwiches again tomorrow, I'm going to jump off this building!'

Then the Scotsman opened his lunch box. 'Oh no!' he moaned. 'Not ham sandwiches again! Every day I get ham sandwiches! If I get ham sandwiches again tomorrow, I'll jump with you!'

The Irishman opened his lunch box and complained: 'Not egg sandwiches again. I don't believe it! Every day it's egg sandwiches without fail! I tell you, if I get egg sandwiches again tomorrow, I'll jump with you!'

The next day the three men sat down for lunch as usual.

The Englishman opened his lunch box, saw that it was cheese sandwiches again and jumped off the building to his death.

The Scotsman opened his box, exclaimed 'Ham again' and jumped off the building.

The Irishman took one look at his sandwiches, saw they were egg again and jumped after the other two.

Since the three men had been friends, there was a triple funeral.

The Englishman's widow sobbed: 'If only I'd known my husband hated cheese.'

The Scotsman's widow wailed: 'And if only I'd known that my husband hated ham.'

The Irishman's widow sighed: 'I just don't understand it. My husband always made his own sandwiches!'

An Englishman, an Irishman and a Scotsman were sitting at a bar. The Englishman said: 'I went into my daughter's room today and found a half-empty bottle of vodka. I didn't even know she drank!'

The Scotsman said: 'That's nothing. I went into my daughter's room today and found a half-empty pack of cigarettes. I didn't even know she smoked!'

The Irishman said: 'That's nothing. I went into my daughter's room today and found a half-empty box of condoms. I didn't even know she was a boy!'

An Englishman, an Irishman and a Scotsman walked into a bar together. They each bought a pint of Guinness but just as they were about to start drinking, three flies landed – one in each of their pints – and became stuck in the thick, creamy head.

The Englishman immediately pushed his pint away in disgust.

The Scotsman fished the fly out of his Guinness and carried on drinking regardless.

The Irishman, too, picked the fly out of his drink, then held it over the beer and yelled at the insect: 'Spit it out! Spit it out, you bastard!'

An Englishman, an Irishman and a Scotsman were walking along a high cliff path when an evil wizard appeared and ordered them to jump off the cliff. To give them a chance of survival, he told them that their landing would be broken by whatever they shouted as they fell.

The Englishman jumped first, shouted 'Pillows', and landed in some nice soft pillows.

The Scotsman went next, shouted 'Hay', and landed in a big soft bale of hay.

The Irishman ran up to the cliff edge but tripped on a rock as he took off. He yelled: 'Oh, sh*t!'

An Englishman, an Irishman and a Scotsman were walking through a field when they came across a cow.

'That's an English cow,' said the Englishman.

'No,' said the Irishman. 'That's definitely an Irish cow.'

'You're both wrong,' said the Scotsman. 'It's clearly a Scottish cow. Look, it's got bagpipes underneath.'

An Englishman, an Irishman and a Scotsman met up at a school reunion.

The Englishman revealed that he had a son. 'He was born on St George's Day, so we called him George.'

'That's funny,' said the Scotsman. 'My son was born on St Andrew's Day, so we called him Andrew.'

'Holy mother of Jesus!' exclaimed the Irishman. 'What a coincidence! Wait till I tell our Pancake!'

An Englishman, an Irishman and a Scotsman were being chased by a police officer. Seeing a deserted warehouse, they ran inside and spotted three empty sacks. Deciding that these were good places to hide they climbed into the sacks.

The police officer entered the warehouse and immediately noticed the three bundles on the floor. He went up to the first one and kicked it. The Englishman inside shouted 'Woof', and the officer, believing it to be a dog, left it.

Then he kicked the second sack, and the Scotsman inside shouted 'Miaow'. Thinking the sack contained a cat, the officer left it.

Finally he kicked the third sack, and the Irishman inside shouted 'Potatoes'.

Two Englishmen, two Irishmen and two Scotsmen were stranded on a desert island. Within days the two Scotsmen had started up a Caledonian Club and were playing the bagpipes and tossing the caber. The two Irishmen started a Céilidh and merrily drank Guinness together every night. But the two Englishmen went to opposite ends of the island and would not speak to each other because they had not been properly introduced.

An Englishman, an Irishman and a Scotsman were driving through the desert when their car broke down. So they got out and started to walk. The Englishman took with him a bottle of wine, the Scotsman took an umbrella and the Irishman took one of the doors off the car.

After a while they came across an old nomad. He said to the Englishman: 'I know why you've got the wine – it's so that you can have a drink when you get thirsty.'

'That's right,' said the Englishman.

Then the nomad said to the Scotsman: 'And I know why you've got the umbrella – it's to keep the sun off you.'

'Aye, you're not wrong,' replied the Scotsman.

'But,' said the nomad, looking at the Irishman, 'I don't understand why you are carrying a car door.'

'Isn't it obvious?' said the Irishman. 'If I get too hot I can wind the window down.'

An Englishman, an Irishman and a Scotsman were discussing the infidelity of their wives.

The Englishman said: 'I think my wife is having an affair with an electrician because last night I found a toolbox under her bed.'

The Scotsman said: 'I think my wife is having an affair with a plumber because last night I found a plunger under her bed.'

The Irishman said: 'And I think my wife is having an affair with a horse because last night I found a jockey under her bed.'

An Englishman, an Irishman and a Scotsman were without tickets for the Summer Olympics but hoped to be able to talk their way in at the stadium gate. Security was very tight, however, and each of their attempts to get in was rejected out of hand.

Wandering around outside the stadium, they came across a construction site. The Englishman had an idea. 'Why don't we take something from the site and pretend to be competitors?'

So the Englishman grabbed a length of scaffolding, announced himself at the stadium gate as 'Jones, pole vault' and was admitted.

Following his lead, the Scotsman picked up a sledge hammer, presented himself at the gate as

'McGregor, hammer' and was allowed in.

Seeing how the ruse had worked for the other two, the Irishman picked up a length of barbed wire, went to the gate and declared: 'O'Malley, fencing.'

An Englishman, an Irishman and a Scotsman applied to join the police force. After passing their written tests, they went in for their interviews with the chief of police.

The Englishman was first. The chief of police said to him: 'I'm going to ask you one question, and if you get it right you can start straight away. Who killed Jesus Christ?'

'That's easy,' said the Englishman. 'Pontius Pilate.'

'Correct,' said the chief. He told the Englishman to go and see the sergeant, who would send him out on traffic duty.

Next was the Scotsman.

'Can you tell me who killed Jesus Christ?' asked the police chief.

'Pontius Pilate,' answered the Scotsman without hesitation and he, too, was sent off to see the sergeant about being put on traffic duty.

Finally it was the Irishman's turn.

'Do you know who killed Jesus Christ?' asked the police chief.

The Irishman thought long and hard and began pacing up and down the room while he thought of an answer. Then he spotted the Englishman and the Scotsman outside in the street directing traffic.

The Irishman protested: 'This is so unfair. They're directing traffic on their first day and I get a murder case to solve!'

An Englishman, an Irishman and a Scotsman agreed to spend six months in three separate locked rooms as part of an experiment. As the Englishman entered his room, he was asked which one item he would like to take with him.

'My wife,' he said. And so he spent six months in the room with his wife.

Next it was the Scotsman's turn and he asked to take a hundred crates of whisky into his room.

Finally, the Irishman was asked what he would like to take into his room. 'A hundred packets of cigarettes,' he answered.

Six months later, the three emerged from their locked rooms. The Englishman came out smiling next to his wife. The Scotsman was so drunk he had to be carried out. Lastly the Irishman came out and asked: 'Has anybody got a light?'

Ethnic Jokes

AMERICAN

An American tourist in an English restaurant had been complaining about everything, particularly the food. When his pork dish arrived, he was so angry that he grabbed the waitress, held out a piece of meat for inspection and growled: 'Here. Do you call that pig?'

The waitress replied sweetly: 'It depends which end of the fork you are referring to, sir.'

A blind Englishman on a flight to Houston found himself seated next to a Texan. The Texan spent the whole trip boasting about how everything is bigger and better in Texas, so that by the time the plane touched down the blind visitor was very excited about his trip.

Exhausted by the journey, the blind man decided to have a drink in his hotel bar before unpacking. He ordered a small soda but the waitress brought a huge glass. As he felt the glass he said: 'Wow! I heard everything is bigger in Texas.'

'It sure is,' said the waitress.

After drinking so much liquid, he needed the bathroom and asked the waitress for directions. She told him to turn right at the end of the bar and to go into the second door on the left. He reached the first door and continued down the hall, but he then stumbled and missed the second door and ended up going through the third door instead. Not realizing he had entered the swimming area, he walked forward and fell into the pool.

Remembering everything he had heard about things being bigger in Texas, as soon as he had his head above water he started shouting: 'Don't flush! Don't flush!'

Why do American eighteen-year-olds take sex education courses?
—So they can learn what they've been doing wrong for the past five years.

What's the best way to pick up American girls?
—With a crane.

What do Americans call a TV set that goes five years without need of repair?
—An import.

Two obese Americans were standing in line at the bank. One said to the other: 'Does chasing the American Dream count as exercise?'

An Englishman said to his friend: 'I started hanging out with this American the other day – not by choice though; I got pulled into his orbit.'

ONLY IN AMERICA

Would they name a state after a bucket of fried chicken.

Can a pizza get to your house faster than an ambulance.

Do people order double cheeseburgers, large fries and a diet Coke.

Do banks leave both doors open and then chain the pens to the counters.

Do they leave cars worth thousands of dollars in the driveway and put their useless junk in the garage.

Are there handicap parking spaces in front of a skating rink.

Do they use answering machines to screen calls and then have call waiting so they won't miss a call from someone they didn't want to talk to in the first place.

AUSTRALIAN

An Englishman wanted to become an Irishman, so he visited a doctor to discuss the procedure. 'It's an extremely delicate operation,' said the doctor, 'and a lot can go wrong. I will have to remove half of your brain.'

'That's okay,' said the Englishman. 'I've always wanted to be Irish so I'm prepared to take the risk.'

The operation went ahead but when the Englishman came round from the anaesthetic, the doctor had a look of horror on his face. 'I'm so sorry,' said the doctor, 'but instead of removing half the brain, I've taken the whole brain out.'

The patient replied: 'No worries, mate!'

Bruce was driving over Sydney Harbour Bridge when he saw his girlfriend about to throw herself off. He slammed on his brakes and shouted: 'Sheila, what do you think you're doing?'

She sobbed: 'Bruce, you got me pregnant, so now I'm going to kill myself.'

Hearing this, Bruce was visibly choked. 'Strewth, Sheila,' he said. 'You're not only a great shag but you're a real sport too.'

Then he drove off.

What's the definition of Australian aristocracy?
—A man who can trace his ancestry back to his father.

What's an Australian's idea of foreplay?
—'You awake, Sheila?'

Why wasn't Jesus born in Sydney?
—They couldn't find three wise men and a virgin.

Why do so many Australian men suffer premature ejaculation?
—Because they have to rush back to the pub to tell their mates what happened.

An Englishman was applying to go and live in Australia.

'Do you have a criminal record?' asked the immigration official.

'No,' said the Englishman. 'Do I need one?'

An Australian guy spotted an attractive woman at a party. He went straight over to her and asked her: Do you want to have sex?'

'Certainly not,' she replied.

'Fair enough,' he said. 'Would you mind lying down while I have some?

IRISH

Paddy was struggling down the road with a heavy wardrobe.

A friend called out: 'Hey, Paddy, why don't you get Mick to help you?'

Paddy said: 'He is. He's inside carrying the clothes.'

How do you get an Irishman to burn his ear?
—Phone him while he's doing the ironing.

How do you spot an Irishman at a car wash?
—He's the one on the bike.

A doctor was explaining to an Irishman how nature automatically adjusts to compensate for some physical disabilities. 'For example,' said the doctor, 'if a man is blind, he often develops a keen sense of touch. If he is deaf, he develops his other senses.'

'I know exactly what you mean,' said the Irishman. 'I've noticed that if a man has one short leg, then the other leg is always a bit longer.'

An Irish decorator was painting a house and the owner arrived home to find him rushing around like a mad thing with his brushes.

'Why are you working so fast?' asked the owner.

'Well, you see, sir,' said the Irish decorator, 'the paint's running low and I want to finish the job before it's all gone.'

Where did they find the Irish woodworm?
—Dead, in a brick.

How do you confuse an Irishman?
—Put three shovels against a wall and tell him to take his pick.

A man went to see a doctor. He prodded himself in the arms, legs and torso with his finger and complained that he was in agony whenever he did that.

'Are you Irish?' asked the doctor.

'Yes, I am,' replied the man.

'I thought so,' said the doctor. 'Your finger is broken.'

What's the difference between an Irish wedding and an Irish funeral?
—One less drunk.

An Irishman took a photograph of his son to be digitally enhanced. He said to the assistant: 'He's wearing a hat in this photo and I'd like you to take it off.'

'That shouldn't be a problem, sir,' said the assistant. 'We can touch it up for you. Tell me, on which side does your son part his hair?'

'Come on now,' said the Irishman. 'You'll see that when you take his hat off!'

SCOTTISH

An English visitor to the Scottish Highlands wanted to smoke and so he asked a passer-by if he could let him have a match.

'Aye, I suppose so,' said the Scotsman, carefully removing one match from his box.

The Englishman rummaged in his jacket pocket and then announced: 'I'm awfully sorry, I seem to have forgotten my cigarettes.'

The Scotsman reached out his hand and said: 'Well, you'll no' be needing the match then.'

What was significant about the Scotsman being run over by a brewery truck?

—It was the first time in his life that the drinks were on him.

How was the Grand Canyon formed?

—A Scotsman on holiday there dropped a dime.

Hamish bought a cheap vase for his sister's birthday but accidentally smashed it before he could give it to her. Rather than go to the expense of buying a replacement present, he decided to gift-wrap the vase, put it in a box and post it to her, intending to claim back the money for the breakage from the postal service.

Three days later, his sister phoned to thank him for the vase but said that it had arrived broken.

'Och, dearie me!' sighed Hamish. 'That's a terrible shame.'

'Yes, isn't it?' said his sister. 'Still, it was very kind of you to wrap each piece individually.'

A Scotsman was on holiday in London and every night he returned to his hotel extolling the virtues of the city.

Eventually another guest asked him: 'Is this your first visit to London?'

'Aye, it is,' replied the Scotsman.

'You seem to be having a great time.'

'Aye. I am that. And it's more than just a holiday – it's my honeymoon as well.'

'Oh really? Where's your wife?'

'Och. She's been here before.'

How do you disperse an angry Scottish mob?
—Pass around a collection bucket.

A woman called on a Scottish friend and found him stripping the wallpaper off the walls.

'Oh, I see you're decorating,' she said.

'No,' he replied. 'I'm moving house.'

Fish

A man went into a fishmonger's carrying a salmon under his arm.

'Do you make fishcakes?' he inquired.

'Yes, we do,' replied the fishmonger.

'Great,' said the man. 'It's his birthday.'

What did the fish say when it hit a concrete wall?
—'Dam!'

Where do shellfish go to borrow money?
—To the prawn broker.

Where do fish keep their money?
—In the river bank.

A country doctor was famous for always catching large fish. One day while he was out on one of his frequent fishing trips he took a call that a woman at a neighbouring farm was giving birth. He rushed to her aid and delivered a healthy baby boy.

Since the farmer had nothing to weigh the baby with, the doctor used his fishing scales. The baby weighed 24lbs 9oz.

Clive and John ordered fish in a restaurant. The waiter brought a dish containing two fish, one noticeably larger than the other.

'Please help yourself,' said Clive to John.

'Okay,' said John, taking the larger fish.

After a brief but tense silence, Clive said: 'You see, if you had offered me the first choice, I would have taken the smaller fish.'

John replied: 'What are you complaining for? You have it, don't you?'

What fish goes up the river at 100mph?
—A motor pike.

What do you get from an angry shark?
—As far away as possible.

Where do you find a down-and-out octopus?
—On squid row.

What kind of money do fishermen make?
—Net profits.

Two fish were in a tank. One turned to the other and said: 'Do you know how to drive one of these things?'

A young boy arrived late for his Sunday school class. Knowing that the boy was usually very prompt, his teacher asked him if anything was wrong. The boy said that he had intended going fishing, but his father had said that he needed to go to church instead.

The teacher was very impressed and asked the boy if his father had explained to him why it was more important to go to church than to go fishing.

'Yes, ma'am, he did,' replied the boy. 'He said that he didn't have enough bait for both of us.'

Two teenagers were fishing in a remote pond when the game warden suddenly jumped out of the bushes. Immediately one of the boys threw down his rod and ran off, hotly pursued by the warden. After about half a mile, the boy stopped to catch his breath and the warden caught up with him.

'Right!' said the warden. 'Let's see your fishing licence, boy!'

With that, the boy pulled out a valid fishing licence and handed it to the warden. 'Well, son,' said the warden scratching his head, 'you must be mighty dumb! You don't have to run from me if you have a valid licence.'

'I know,' replied the boy. 'But you see, my friend back there, he don't have one...'

A priest was walking along the cliffs at Dover when he came upon two locals pulling another man ashore on the end of a rope.

'That's what I like to see,' said the priest. 'Man helping his fellow man.'

As the priest walked away, one local remarked to the other: 'Well, he sure doesn't know the first thing about shark fishing.'

Food

A wife served some homemade apple tarts after dinner and waited eagerly for her husband's comments. When he said nothing, she asked: 'If I baked these commercially, how much do you think I would get for them?'

Without batting an eyelid, he answered: 'About fifteen years.'

A beggar walked up to a smart woman in the street and said: 'I haven't eaten anything in three days.'

'Gosh,' she said. 'I wish I had your willpower.'

Two male students were moaning about how expensive it was living on takeaway meals.

'I do own a cookery book,' said one, 'but I've never been able to use it.'

'Why not?' asked the other. 'Are the recipes too difficult?'

'I don't think so but each one started the same way: take a clean dish ...'

A wife asked her husband to go to the supermarket and buy some organic vegetables. Unable to find any on the shelves, he asked a male employee for assistance.

'These vegetables are for my wife,' said the customer. 'Have they been sprayed with poisonous chemicals?'

'No,' replied the employee. 'You'll have to do that yourself!'

A man said to his friend: 'My wife is on a new diet – coconuts and bananas. She hasn't lost any weight but, boy, can she climb a tree now!'

How do you make an apple crumble?
—Torture it for twenty minutes.

A man arrived home from work to find his wife being particularly attentive. 'How were your sandwiches today, darling?' she inquired.

'They were very tasty,' he replied.

'Are you sure they were okay?' she asked again.

'Yes, they were fine.'

'They didn't make you feel ill at all then?'

'No. Why do you ask?'

'Oh, no reason. It's just that tomorrow you'll have to clean your shoes with fish paste.'

Did you hear about the man who lost consciousness after eating a curry?
—He was left in a korma.

Good King Wenceslas went into his local pizza parlour.

'What sort of pizza would you like?' asked the sales assistant.

Good King Wenceslas said: 'Deep pan, crisp and even.'

A woman returned home from her regular coffee afternoon with her friends and realized that she had nothing for her husband's dinner. All she could find in the pantry was a tin of cat food, an egg and a lettuce leaf. With no time to go shopping, she stirred the egg into the cat food, cooked it and served it garnished with the lettuce leaf.

A few minutes later her hungry husband arrived home from work, ate the meal and said it was the best thing she had ever cooked.

At the following week's coffee afternoon, she told her friends that her husband's favourite meal was now cat food. 'He has had egg and cat food every day for the past week, and he absolutely loves it.'

'You can't feed him cat food,' said the others. 'You'll kill him.'

Sure enough, two weeks later the woman sadly informed her friends that her husband had died.

'We told you that giving him cat food would kill him!' they said.

'It had nothing to do with the cat food,' she replied. 'He died when he fell off the garden fence.'

'What was he doing up there?' they asked.

The woman said: 'He was trying to lick his backside.'

How does Bob Marley like his doughnuts?
—Wi' jammin.

What happened to the man who went to a seafood disco?
—He pulled a mussel.

A customer in a restaurant asked for some two-handed cheese.

'Two-handed cheese?' queried the waiter. 'What do you mean?'

'You know,' the customer explained, 'the kind you eat with one hand and hold your nose with the other.'

Two Korean tourists arrived in Washington and were surprised to see a street vendor selling hot dogs. 'I never knew Americans also ate dogs,' said one. 'Let's see what they're like.'

So they ordered hot dogs and sat down on a park bench to eat them. But when the first Korean opened his bun and looked inside, he was horrified. 'I'm not eating that!' he exclaimed. 'That's disgusting!' Turning to his friend, he said: 'What part of the dog did you get?'

When the power went off at the local primary school, the cook couldn't serve a hot meal in the cafeteria. She had to feed the children something, so at the last minute she whipped up great stacks of peanut butter sandwiches.

As one little boy filled his plate, he said: 'It's about time. At last, a home-cooked meal.'

Two peanuts were walking down the road. One was assaulted.

On a sudden whim, a man decided to take his family out for a meal. The bill came to more than he had expected, so at the end of the meal he asked the waiter: 'Could I have a bag to take the leftovers home for the dog?'

Hearing this, his young daughter said excitedly: 'Hey, Dad, are we getting a dog?'

Health and Fitness

A man decided to take a long hot bath after a stressful week at work. As soon as he climbed into the bath tub his doorbell rang. He climbed out of the tub, wrapped himself in a large towel, put on his slippers and went downstairs to answer the door. It was a salesman selling brushes. The man slammed the door and went back to his hot bath.

A few minutes later the doorbell rang again. He climbed out of the tub again, wrapped himself in the large towel, wrapped a small towel around his head, put on his slippers and went downstairs to answer the door. It was an energy company wanting the man to change supplier. The man slammed the door again and went back to his bath.

After five minutes the doorbell rang again. He climbed out of the bath, put on his slippers and wrapped himself in the towels, but as he walked across the bathroom floor he slipped on a wet patch and fell against the porcelain bath tub, injuring himself.

He struggled into his clothes, gingerly climbed into his car and, in great pain, drove himself to the doctor's surgery. The doctor examined him and said: 'You're lucky, there are no bones broken. But you do need to relax. Why don't you go home and take a long, hot bath?'

A man phoned his local gym and said: 'I want you to teach me how to do the splits.'

The gym assistant asked: 'How flexible are you?'

The man said: 'I can't make Tuesdays or Thursdays.'

An obese woman was run over by a car driver.

Her distraught husband wailed: 'Surely you must have seen her! Couldn't you have avoided her?'

The motorist said: 'Sure I saw her but I didn't have enough petrol to drive round her.'

Two young boys were discussing their respective illnesses in the hospital children's ward. 'Are you medical or surgical?' asked one boy who had been in for several days.

'What's the difference?' asked the other.

'It's simple. Were you sick when you came in or did they make you sick when you got here?'

A woman phoned 999 to report that her mother had fallen down the stairs.

'Do you know what caused her to fall?' asked the emergency operator.

'No,' replied the woman. 'What?'

Jim worked in a small pharmacy but he was not much of a salesman. He could never find the item the customer wanted. Bob the owner was beginning to lose patience and warned Jim that the next sale he missed would be his last. Just then a man came into the pharmacy coughing. He asked for the best cough syrup but, try as he might, Jim was unable to find it. Remembering his boss's warning, he sold the man a box of Ex-Lax and told him to take it all at once.

Bob had witnessed the whole thing and went over to Jim to ask what had happened. Jim explained: 'He wanted something for his cough but I couldn't find the cough syrup. So I sold him Ex-Lax instead.'

'Ex-Lax won't cure a cough,' shouted Bob angrily.

'Sure it will,' said Jim, pointing to the man leaning against the lamp-post. 'Look at him; he is afraid to cough.'

A brown paper bag went to the doctor and complained of feeling unwell. After carrying out a series of tests, the doctor asked the bag to come back in seven days.

When the bag returned, the doctor said: 'I'm afraid I have some bad news. We discovered from your blood tests that you have haemophilia.'

'That's impossible! How can I have haemophilia? I'm a brown paper bag.'

'Yes,' said the doctor, 'but your mother was a carrier.'

A man confessed to his doctor: 'Last night I was going to kill myself by swallowing a handful of aspirins.'

'What happened to make you change your mind?' asked the doctor.

'After taking two I felt much better.'

A young man was lying in a hospital bed, his entire body swathed in bandages.

The guy in the next bed asked: 'What's your line of work?'

'I'm a former window cleaner.'

'Oh, when did you give it up?'

The young man said: 'About halfway down.'

There are warnings of a new disease found in soft butter. Apparently it spreads easily!

Kevin went to the doctor and announced: 'Doc, I want to be castrated.'

'What on earth for?' asked the doctor in amazement.

Kevin replied: 'It's something I've been thinking about for a long time and I really want it done.'

'But have you thought it through properly?' said the doctor. 'It's an extremely serious operation and once it's done there's no going back. It will change your life forever.'

'I realize that,' said Kevin, 'but you're not going to get me to change my mind. Either you book me in to be castrated or I'll go to another doctor.'

'Very well,' said the doctor reluctantly. 'But it's against my better judgement.'

So Kevin had the operation and the following day he was walking very gingerly, legs apart, down the hospital corridor. Heading towards him was another patient who was walking exactly the same way.

'Hi,' said Kevin. 'It looks as though you've just had the same operation as me.'

'Well,' said the other patient, 'I finally decided at the age of forty-one that I wanted to be circumcized.'

Kevin looked at him in horror and yelled: 'Damn! That's the word!'

A man visited his optician and said: 'I keep seeing spots in front of my eyes.'

'Have you seen a doctor?'

'No, just the spots!'

A man went into a drugstore and asked the pharmacist if he could give him something for hiccups. Without warning, the pharmacist came round from behind the counter and punched the man hard in the stomach.

'What did you do that for?' gasped the man.

'Well, you haven't got hiccups anymore, have you?' said the pharmacist.

'No,' replied the man, 'but my wife still has!'

Heaven and Hell

Three nuns died in a car crash but when they arrived in heaven they found it closed for repairs. Eventually St Peter appeared, apologized for the inconvenience and told them that while the repair work was being completed, they could return to Earth for two days as anyone they wished. 'Then when we re-open we will accept you into heaven.'

'That sounds fair,' said the first nun who said she would like to return to Earth as Joan of Arc 'because she gave her life to God'.

'That's okay,' said St Peter. 'You can go back as Joan of Arc.'

The second nun said she wanted to go back to

Earth as Mother Theresa 'because she selflessly devoted herself to others'.

'No problem,' said St Peter. 'You can go back as Mother Theresa.'

The third nun announced: 'I want to go back as Alice Kapipelean.'

'Who?' queried St Peter.

'Alice Kapipelean,' repeated the nun.

'I'm sorry,' said St Peter, looking through his list of names, 'but we have no record of any Alice Kapipelean being on Earth.'

'There must be some mistake,' insisted the nun, handing a newspaper cutting to St Peter. 'See, I have proof right here.'

St Peter glanced at the cutting. 'No, Sister,' he smiled. 'You have misread the article. It says that the Alaska Pipeline was laid by five hundred men in six months!'

A man approached the Pearly Gates and asked to be admitted into heaven.

'I can only allow you into heaven if you have performed a good deed,' said St Peter.

'I have,' replied the man. 'I once saved a young woman from a gang of Hell's Angels. I ran my car over their bikes, then got out and pulled the leader hard by his ponytail until he let the girl go.'

'Really?' said St Peter. 'That's strange. The incident doesn't seem to be in our records. When did it happen?'

The man said: 'About five minutes ago.'

Three men died in an accident on Christmas Eve. Presenting themselves at the Pearly Gates, they were informed by St Peter that, in order to gain admission, they had to produce something related to Christmas.

The first man rummaged through his pocket and found some mistletoe, so he was allowed in.

The second man waved a cracker, so he was allowed in.

The third man pulled out a pair of ladies' knickers.

'How do these represent Christmas?' asked St Peter.

The man replied: 'They're Carol's.'

Chris and Sam were inseparable childhood friends but one night they both died in a motorbike accident. When Chris woke up in heaven, he began to search for Sam but couldn't find him anywhere. Distraught, he went to St Peter and said: 'I know Sam died with me in the bike smash but I can't find him up here.'

'I'm sorry,' said St Peter, 'but Sam didn't make it to heaven. He's gone to hell instead.'

The news upset Chris so much that he begged St Peter to let him see his friend one last time. So St Peter parted the clouds and Chris saw Sam sitting in hell with a keg of beer on one side and a beautiful, buxom woman on the other.

Chris looked at St Peter and said: 'Are you sure I'm in the right place?'

'Looks can be deceiving, my son,' said St Peter. 'You see that keg of beer? It has a hole in it. You see that woman? She doesn't!'

A woman was worried that her dead husband might not have made it to heaven, so she decided to try and contact him through a séance. Soon her husband's voice was heard: 'Hello, Margaret, it's me, George.'

'George,' said the wife, 'I just need to know that you're happy in the afterlife. What's it like there?'

'It's more beautiful than I ever imagined,' answered George. 'The sky is bluer, the air is cleaner, and the pastures are much more lush and green than I ever expected. And all we do each day is eat and sleep.'

'Thank goodness you made it to heaven,' said the wife.

'Heaven?' said George. 'What do you mean heaven? I'm a buffalo in Montana.'

Facing death, an extremely wealthy man was reluctant to leave his worldly goods behind on Earth and prayed that he might be able to take them with him to heaven. An angel heard his plea and told him that, after much discussion, God would allow him to bring one suitcase.

Overjoyed, the man fetched his biggest suitcase and filled it with solid gold bars. A week later, the man died and turned up at the Pearly Gates carrying his suitcase.

St Peter took one look at the suitcase and said: 'I'm sorry, you can't bring that in here. We don't allow suitcases.'

The man explained that God had granted him special dispensation to bring one suitcase. After verifying the story, St Peter said: 'Before you can come in, I must check the contents.' So he opened the suitcase to inspect the worldly items that the man found too precious to leave behind. As the lid sprang back to reveal the gold bars, St Peter exclaimed: 'You brought pavement?!'

Three men were standing in line hoping to enter heaven. St Peter appeared and told the first man: 'I'm sorry but we've been really busy lately and the place is nearly full, so I can only admit people who have suffered particularly horrible deaths. So what's your story?'

The first man replied: 'For some time now I've suspected that my wife has been cheating on me, so this morning I sneaked home from work to try and catch her red-handed. As I came into our thirty-first-floor apartment, I could tell something was wrong. I searched everywhere but I couldn't find where her lover was hiding. Then I stepped out on to the balcony and saw this guy hanging from the railings thirty-one floors above the ground. By now I was really mad, so I started hitting and kicking him, but somehow he still managed to cling on. Finally I went back into the apartment, fetched a hammer and hammered on his fingers until at last he let go and fell. But wouldn't you know it, his fall was broken by some bushes! I was so angry about him surviving that I picked up the fridge and hurled it at him, and it struck him on the head, killing him instantly. But the stress of hurling the fridge proved too much for me and I suffered a heart attack and died there on the balcony.'

'That sounds like a pretty bad day to me,' said St Peter, and he let the man in.

Then the second man stepped forward. St Peter explained about heaven being almost full and asked him for his story.

'I've had a really odd day,' began the second man. 'You see, I live on the thirty-second floor of a high-rise block and every morning I do my exercises out on the balcony. Well, this morning I must have slipped because I fell over the edge. Luckily I caught the railing of the balcony on the floor below me. I was hanging on for dear life when this guy suddenly burst out on to the balcony. I thought he was going to rescue me but instead he started hitting and kicking me. I held on the best I could until he ran into his apartment, grabbed a hammer and started pounding on my hands. Eventually I just let go but again I got lucky and fell into some bushes. Just when I thought I was going to be okay, a refrigerator came crashing out of the sky, hit me on the head and that's how I ended up here.'

'That's a pretty horrible death,' said St Peter, and he allowed the man into heaven.

Then the third man stepped forward. St Peter explained that heaven was nearly full and asked him for his story.

'Picture this,' said the third man. 'I'm hiding inside a refrigerator ...'

On his death, a man was despatched to hell. There, Satan showed him the doors to three rooms and told him that he had to choose one of the rooms in which to spend eternity.

The man opened the first door and saw people standing up to their shoulders in cow manure. 'I don't fancy that,' said the man. 'What's in the next room?'

Satan showed him the second room, where people were standing up to their noses in cow manure. 'No way!' exclaimed the man. 'What's in the third room?'

So Satan showed him the third room. Here people were standing around drinking cups of tea and eating cakes, with cow manure up to their knees.

'I'll choose this room,' said the man.

'Very well,' said Satan. 'In you go.'

As he closed the door behind him, Satan called out: 'Okay, you lot. Tea break's over. Back on your heads!'

A woman died and went to heaven. On her first day there she asked St Peter: 'Please can I be reunited with my dear departed husband? He died fourteen years ago.'

'I'll try,' said St Peter. 'What's his name?'

'John Smith,' replied the woman.

'Unfortunately that's a very common name,' said St Peter, 'so it might not be easy to find him. But sometimes we can identify people by their last words. Do you happen to remember what they were?'

She replied: 'He said that if I ever slept with another man after he was gone, he would turn in his grave.'

'Oh,' said St Peter. 'You mean Spinning John Smith!'

Hearing a knock at the doors of the Pearly Gates, St Peter looked out and saw a man standing there but by the time he had opened the gates the man had vanished.

St Peter went back inside but a few moments later there was another knock and the same man was standing there. St Peter opened the gates but again the man had disappeared.

St Peter had just settled down again when there was a third knock. Wearily he opened the gates to find the same man standing there.

'Are you messing me about?' asked St Peter.

'No,' said the man. 'They're trying to resuscitate me.'

Three women friends died in an accident and went to heaven. Meeting them at the Pearly Gates, St Peter said: 'There is one rule you must remember here – don't step on the ducks.'

Once inside, they saw that heaven was littered with ducks and the first woman accidentally trod on one immediately. St Peter quickly appeared with the ugliest man the woman had ever seen and told her: 'Your punishment for stepping on a duck is to spend eternity chained to this man.'

A few hours later, the second woman trod on a duck and she, too, found herself chained to a hideous looking man as punishment.

Seeing the fate that had befallen her friends, the third woman took great care not to step on any ducks. Then one day St Peter appeared and chained her to an extremely handsome young man. The woman couldn't believe her good fortune and, feeling blessed, asked St Peter why the young man had been chained to her.

St Peter replied: 'He trod on a duck.'

A man died and went to hell. He was feeling sorry for himself until the Devil appeared and said: 'Why are you looking so glum? We have a great time down here.'

'Really?' said the man.

'Yes, really,' said the Devil. 'Do you drink?'

'Sure I drink. I used to love hanging out in bars.'

'Well, you're going to love Mondays,' laughed the Devil. 'On Mondays all we do is drink – beer, whisky, whatever you want, and as much as you can take. Tell me, do you smoke?'

'Sure I do,' replied the man.

'Then you're going to love Tuesdays,' said the Devil. 'We have the finest cigars flown in from Cuba and we smoke all day long. I bet you like to gamble?'

'Who doesn't!' exclaimed the man.

'Well, you're going to love Wednesdays,' said the Devil. 'We have our own casino – poker, roulette, blackjack, the lot. Do you do drugs?'

'Sure, I do drugs,' said the man.

'Then you're going to love Thursdays,' said the Devil, 'because Thursday is drug day. You can do all the drugs you want without any cops to worry about.'

'Hey,' said the man, 'I never realized hell was such a great place.'

'Well, we aim to please,' said the Devil. 'And I bet you're gay, too, huh?'

'No, I'm not,' said the man.

'That's a real shame,' said the Devil. 'You're going to hate Fridays.'

Law and Order

A police officer spotted a Harley speeding through San Francisco, so he pulled over the biker and asked for his name.

'Jake,' he replied.

'Jake what?' asked the officer.

'Just Jake,' said the biker.

'Listen, pal,' said the officer. 'It's a nice day so I'm going to let you off with a warning.'

'Thanks, Officer.'

'But come on, what is your last name?'

'I lost it.'

'What do you mean you lost it?' asked the officer, by now convinced that he was dealing with a crank. 'How did you lose it?'

'Okay, I'll tell you. It's a long story, so stay with me. I was born Jake Johnson. I studied hard and got good grades. As I got older, I decided I wanted to be a doctor. I went through college, medical school, internship, residence, and finally got my degree, so I was Jake Johnson, MD. But after a while I got bored with being a doctor, so I went back to school and studied dentistry instead. I got all the way through school, got my degree, and so I was Jake Johnson, MD, DDS. But I got bored doing dentistry and started fooling around with my assistant and she gave me VD. So now I was Jake Johnson, MD, DDS, with VD. Well, the ADA found out about the VD, so they took away my DDS. Then I was Jake Johnson, MD, with VD. Then the AMA found out about the ADA taking away my DDS because of the VD, so they took away my MD, leaving me as Jake Johnson with VD. Then the VD took away my Johnson, so now I am just Jake.'

A husband and his wife were driving home from the bar one night when he got pulled over by the police. The officer told him that he was stopped because his left rear brake light was out.

The husband said: 'I'm very sorry, Officer, I didn't realize it was out. I'll get it fixed right away.'

His wife interrupted: 'I knew this would happen when I told you two days ago to get that light fixed.'

'Shut up,' said the husband.

Next, the officer asked for the husband's licence and after looking at it said: 'Sir, your licence has expired.'

Again the husband apologized and added that he didn't realize that it had expired and would take care of it first thing in the morning.

The wife butted in: 'I told you a week ago that you'd received a letter telling you that your license had expired.'

By this time, the husband was becoming really annoyed that his wife was repeatedly contradicting him in front of the officer and he said loudly: 'Shut your mouth, you stupid woman!'

The officer then leaned over towards the wife and asked: 'Does your husband always talk to you like that?'

She replied: 'Only when he's drunk.'

A man walked into his local sheriff's office and announced: 'I'd like to become a deputy.'

'Good, I want you to catch this guy,' said the sheriff, handing the man a Wanted poster.

The poster read: Last seen wearing a brown

paper hat, brown paper shirt, brown paper pants and brown paper boots.

'What's he wanted for?' asked the aspiring deputy.

The sheriff replied: 'Rustling.'

A man was racing down a Louisiana highway, feeling secure in a group of cars all travelling at the same speed. However, as they passed a speed trap, he got nailed by an infrared detector and was forced to pull over.

He said to the cop: 'Listen, Officer, I know I was speeding but I don't think it's fair. There were plenty of other cars around me who were going just as fast, so why should I be the one to get a ticket?'

'Ever go fishing?' asked the cop.

'Uh, yeah,' replied the man, bewildered by the line of questioning.

The cop grinned and added: 'Did you ever catch 'em all?'

A police officer who was working nights at the station was relieved of duty early one night and arrived home four hours earlier than usual, at around 2am.

Not wanting to wake his wife, he undressed in the dark, crept into the bedroom and started to climb into bed. But just as he was about to do so, his wife sat up in bed and said: 'Dan, would you go down to the all-night drugstore on the next block to get me some aspirin? I've got a splitting headache.'

'Sure, honey,' he said, and feeling his way across the dark room he got dressed and made his way to the drugstore.

When he entered the drug store, the pharmacist looked up in surprise. 'I know you,' said the pharmacist. 'Aren't you a policeman? Officer Kendall?'

'Yeah,' said the officer. 'So?'

'Well, what the heck are you doing all dressed up like the Fire Chief?'

A small-town prosecuting attorney called his first witness to the stand in a trial – a grandmother in her eighties. He approached her and asked: 'Mrs Brown, do you know me?'

She responded: 'Why, yes, I do know you, Mr Collins. I've known you since you were a young boy. And frankly, you've been a big disappointment to me. You lie, you cheat on your wife, you manipulate people and talk about them behind their backs. You think you're a rising big shot when you haven't the brains to realize you never will amount to anything more than a two-bit paper pusher. Yes, I know you.'

The lawyer was stunned. Not knowing what else to do he pointed across the room and asked: 'Mrs Brown, do you know the defence attorney?'

She replied: 'Why, yes I do. I've known Mr Ferris since he was a youngster, too. I used to babysit him for his parents. And he, too, has been a real disappointment to me. He's lazy, bigoted and he has a drinking problem. The man can't build a normal relationship with anyone and his law practice is one of the shoddiest in the entire state. Yes, I know him.'

At this point, the judge rapped the courtroom to silence and called both attorneys to the bench. In a very quiet voice, he said with menace: 'If either of you asks her if she knows me, you'll be jailed for contempt.'

A police officer attended the scene of a fatal road smash. He arrived to find the driver's decapitated head lying in the middle of the road.

Taking out his notebook to record the scene, he wrote: 'Head on bullevard.' Then he scratched out his spelling error and wrote: 'Head on bouelevard.' Again, realizing the spelling was incorrect, he scratched it out.

Finally when he was sure that nobody was

looking, he kicked the head to one side and wrote in his notebook: 'Head in gutter.'

When a police station got two new horses, two cops were assigned to be mounted policemen. They went off for a ride and came back pleased with the new acquisitions.

'This horse is great,' said the first cop. 'I'm always going to take this one.'

'My horse is great, too,' said the second cop. 'From now on, I'm always going to take it. The only problem is, how do we know which horse is which?'

They thought for a minute and then the first cop came up with an idea. 'I know,' he said. 'Let's cut off this one's tail.'

The second cop agreed and the horse lost its tail.

The next morning the police chief was inspecting the horses. He was in an angry mood.

'What's wrong?' asked the two cops.

'What's wrong!' bellowed the chief. 'I'll tell you what's wrong! You two morons cut off the horse's tail – that's what's wrong!'

'But chief,' they protested, 'it was the only way we could tell the two horses apart.'

'What are you talking about?' yelled the chief. 'Can't you see that the black one is a bit taller than the white one?!'

Lawyers

A doctor was spending time on the beach with his family. Suddenly the doctor spotted a dorsal fin sticking out of the water and collapsed. When he came to, his wife said: 'You have to be less paranoid, dear. That was only a shark. Stop imagining there are lawyers everywhere.'

A doctor and a lawyer were talking at a party. However, their conversation was constantly interrupted by people describing their ailments and asking the doctor for free medical advice.

After an hour of this, the exasperated doctor asked the lawyer: 'What do you do to stop people from asking you for legal advice when you're out of the office?'

'I give it to them,' replied the lawyer, 'and then I send them a bill.'

The doctor was shocked but agreed to give it a try. The next day, still feeling slightly guilty, the doctor prepared the bills and then went out to mail them. On his way out he checked his postbox and found a bill from the lawyer!

Two cars were involved in a collision. One was driven by a lawyer, the other by an accountant. Seeing that the accountant had been shaken up by the incident, the lawyer offered him a drink from his hip flask.

'That's very kind of you,' said the accountant, taking a swig from the flask before handing it back to the lawyer. 'Aren't you having one yourself?'

'Sure,' said the lawyer, 'but I'll wait until after the police have gone.'

What do you call three thousand dead lawyers at the bottom of the ocean?
—A start.

How do you get a lawyer down from a tree?
—Cut the rope.

What do you call a lawyer with an IQ of sixty?
—Your Honour.

What's the difference between a lawyer and a catfish?
—One's a scum-sucking bottom dweller, the other's a fish.

Why are lawyers buried in twenty-foot holes?
—Because deep down they're all really nice guys.

A lawyer and an engineer were fishing in the Caribbean. The lawyer said: 'I'm here because my house burned down and everything I owned was destroyed by the fire. The insurance company paid for everything.'

'That's amazing,' said the engineer. 'I'm here because my house and all of my belongings were destroyed by a flood and my insurance company also paid for everything.'

The lawyer looked somewhat confused and asked: 'How do you start a flood?'

A man went into a pet shop to buy a parrot. The shop owner pointed to three identical-looking parrots on a perch and said: 'The parrot on the left costs five hundred pounds.'

'Why does the parrot cost so much?' asked the customer.

The owner said: 'Well, the parrot knows how to do legal research.'

'What about the next parrot?' said the customer. 'How much is that?'

'That costs one thousand pounds,' said the owner, 'because it can do everything the other parrot can do plus it knows how to write a brief that will win any case.'

The customer was staggered by the prices. 'How much is the third parrot?' he asked.

'Four thousand pounds,' replied the owner.

'Four thousand pounds! What can it do to be so expensive?'

The owner replied: 'To be honest, I've never seen her do a thing but the other two call her Senior Partner.'

The bad-tempered senior partner in a firm of lawyers passed away but his office kept receiving calls asking to speak to him. At least three times a day the receptionist had to inform callers: 'I'm sorry, Paul Taylor is dead.'

After two weeks of this it finally dawned on the receptionist that it was the same person making all the calls. So the next time the voice rang asking to speak to Paul Taylor, she said: 'Who are you and why do you carry on calling? I keep telling you, Paul Taylor is dead.'

'I know,' said the caller. 'But I used to be one of his junior associates and I just like hearing you say it.'

A Hindu priest, a Rabbi and a lawyer were driving down the road when their car broke down. They found a farmhouse nearby but the farmer informed them that he had only one spare room with just two twin beds so someone would have to sleep in the barn.

After much discussion, the Hindu volunteered to go to the barn. A few moments later, there was a knock on the bedroom door. The Hindu explained that there was a cow in the barn and, as cows are sacred, he could not possibly sleep in the barn with a cow.

Although annoyed by the development, the Rabbi volunteered to sleep in the barn. A few moments later, there was a knock on the door. The Rabbi explained that there was a pig in the barn and that he, being very orthodox, could not possibly spend the evening in the barn with the origin of pork.

Finally, the lawyer said that he would go to the

barn. A few moments later there was a knock on the door. It was the cow and the pig.

An engineer died and went to heaven. However, when St Peter met him at the Pearly Gates he said: 'Wait a minute! You're in the wrong place. Beat it!'

So the engineer went down to hell and soon got settled in. But he quickly became dissatisfied with conditions there and began to make improvements. Before long, there was running water, flush toilets, escalators and even air conditioning! The engineer was a pretty popular guy.

One day God phoned Satan and said with a sneer: 'So, how is it going down there?'

Satan replied: 'Hey, things are going great. We've got running water, flush toilets, escalators, air conditioning, and there's no telling what this engineer is going to come up with next.'

'What, you've got an engineer?' said God. 'That's a mistake – he should never have gone down there. Send him up right away!'

'No way!' said Satan. 'I like having an engineer on the staff, I'm keeping him.'

God insisted: 'Send him up here or I'll sue you!'

'Oh, yeah?' replied Satan. 'Where are you going to find a lawyer?!'

Light Bulb Jokes

How many actors does it take to change a light bulb?
—One: they don't like to share the spotlight.

How many Australians does it take to change a light bulb?
—Two. One to hold the bulb and one to drink until the room spins.

How many economists does it take to screw in a light bulb?
—None. If the light bulb really needed changing, market forces would already have caused it to happen.

How many civil servants does it take to change a light bulb?

—Fifty-eight. One to change the bulb and fifty-seven to do the paperwork.

How many divorced men does it take to screw in a light bulb?

—Who knows? They never get to keep the house.

How many folk singers does it take to change a light bulb?

—Two. One to change the bulb and the other to write a song about how good the old bulb was.

How many real men does it take to change a light bulb?

—None. Real men aren't afraid of the dark.

How many Jewish mothers does it take to change a light bulb?

—None. 'Don't worry about me, I'll just sit here in the dark ...'

How many mechanics does it take to change a light bulb?

—Three. One to scratch his head, one to say it won't be ready until next Thursday and one to tally up the bill.

How many existentialists does it take to change a light bulb?
—Two. One to screw it in and the other to observe how the light bulb symbolizes a single, incandescent beacon of subjective reality in a netherworld of endless absurdity.

How many mothers-in-law does it take to change a light bulb?
—Fifty. One to change it and the other forty-nine to say, 'I told you so!'

How many movie directors does it take to change a light bulb?
—One, but he'll want to do it sixteen times.

How many police officers does it take to screw in a light bulb?
—None. It turned itself in.

How many movie stars does it take to change a light bulb?
—One. He holds it and waits for the world to revolve around him.

How many nihilists does it take to change a light bulb?
—There is nothing to change.

How many pessimists does it take to change a light bulb?

—None. The old one is probably screwed in too tight.

How many politicians does it take to change a light bulb?

—None. Politicians only promise change.

How many psychiatrists does it take to change a light bulb?

—One, but the bulb has really got to want to change.

How many women with PMS does it take to change a light bulb?

—None. 'You can damn well do it yourself!'

Marriage and Divorce

'I bet you don't know what day this is,' said the wife to her husband as he was about to leave for work one morning.

The husband was seized with panic but, doing his best to appear unruffled, replied: 'Of course I do, darling. How could I forget?'

With that he rushed off to catch his train.

At eleven o'clock that morning the wife was delighted to open the door and find a delivery man waiting with a huge box of chocolates.

At one o'clock another delivery arrived – this time a dozen red roses.

Then at four o'clock came a third delivery – a

beautiful designer evening dress ordered from an exclusive boutique.

The wife could hardly wait for her husband to arrive home. He in turn was feeling smug that he had extricated himself from a potentially sticky situation.

As he walked through the door, she threw her arms around him and said joyously: 'First the chocolates, then the roses and then the dress. This has to be the best Shrove Tuesday ever!'

A man and a woman were sitting at a restaurant table when the man suddenly slid off his chair and disappeared under the table. The woman seemed unconcerned but a waitress, who had seen what had happened, thought she ought to say something.

'Excuse me, madam,' she said. 'I think your husband just slid under the table.'

'No,' replied the woman frostily. 'My husband just walked in the door.'

A month after her wedding, an anxious new bride called her priest.

'Father,' she said, 'Paul and I had a terrible fight.

It was really bad. I just don't know what to do next.'

'Try not to worry,' said the priest. 'All couples have their first fight.'

'Yes, I know that,' she said. 'But what am I going to do with the body?'

A man revealed to his work colleagues that, on a romantic impulse, he had asked his girlfriend to marry him.

'What did she say?' asked one.

'I don't know,' he said. 'She hasn't emailed me back yet.'

A little boy was attending his first wedding. After the service, his cousin asked him: 'How many women can a man marry?'

'Sixteen,' the boy responded.

His cousin was amazed that he had an answer so quickly. 'How do you know that?' he asked.

'Easy,' said the little boy. 'All you have to do is add it up, like the vicar said: four better, four worse, four richer, four poorer.'

A man arrived home after an exhausting day at the office, flopped down on the sofa in front of the television and called to his wife: 'Fetch me a beer before it starts.'

The wife muttered darkly and brought him a beer.

Ten minutes later, he called out: 'Fetch me another beer before it starts.'

She fetched another beer and angrily threw it to him.

Five minutes later, he yelled: 'Quick, get me another beer. It's going to start any minute.'

This was too much for the wife to take. 'Is that all you're going to do all evening?' she screamed. 'Drink beer and sit in front of the TV? You're just a lazy, fat, drunken slob who's …'

The husband sighed: 'It's started …'

A devoted wife had spent her lifetime caring for her husband, so when he spent several months in a coma she was there at his side in hospital every day.

Eventually he came round and, in a weak voice, said to her: 'You have been with me through all the bad times. When I got fired from my job, you were there for me. When my business failed, you were there. When I had a heart attack, you were there, too. When I got shot, you were by my side. You know what?'

'What, darling?' his wife asked gently.

'I reckon you've brought me nothing but bad luck.'

A new bride was embarrassed at being recognized as a honeymooner. So as she and her husband pulled up to the hotel, she turned to him and said: 'Is there a way we can make it look as if we've been married a long time?'

'Sure,' he said. 'You carry the suitcases.'

A woman with thirteen children, aged between one and thirteen, sued her husband for divorce on the grounds of desertion.

'When did he desert you?' inquired the judge.

'Twelve years ago,' answered the woman.

'I don't understand,' said the judge. 'If he left you twelve years ago, where did all the children come from?'

'He kept coming back to say he was sorry.'

Two husbands were drowning their sorrows in a bar. One said: 'Why do you and your wife fight all the time?'

'I don't know,' replied the other. 'She never tells me.'

A recently wed husband returned home from work to be greeted by his wife. 'I have some wonderful news for you, darling,' she announced excitedly. 'Pretty soon there's going to be three of us in this house instead of two. There's going to be another mouth to feed.'

'That's fantastic,' he beamed, relishing the prospect of fatherhood.

'I'm glad you feel that way,' said his wife, 'because mother moves in with us tomorrow.'

A wife arrived home to find her husband in bed with another woman. With superhuman strength borne out of fury, she dragged him down the stairs to the garage and put his manhood in a vice. She then secured it tightly, removed the handle and picked up a hacksaw.

The husband screamed in terror: 'You're not going to cut it off, are you?'

'No, I'm not,' she grinned. 'You are. I'm going to set the garage on fire.'

A wife was feeling neglected and wanted to know how much her husband loved her. 'If I were to die tomorrow,' she said, 'and you remarried, would you give your new wife my jewellery?'

'What a terrible thing to ask!' exclaimed the husband. 'But no, of course I wouldn't.'

'And would you give her any of my clothes?'

'No, honey, of course I wouldn't. I can't believe you're even asking me a question like that.'

'What about my golf clubs?' said the wife.

'No,' replied the husband emphatically. 'She's left-handed.'

A man was talking to his best friend about married life. 'I really trust my wife,' he said, 'and I'm pretty sure she's always been faithful to me. But there's always that doubt.'

'Yes, I know what you mean,' said the friend. 'I guess it's the same in a lot of marriages.'

A month later, the man had to go away for a few days on a business trip but before leaving he asked his friend: 'While I'm away could you do me a favour and keep an eye on my house, just in case there's anything suspicious going on? Don't get me wrong, I trust my wife implicitly. But there's always that doubt.'

The friend agreed to watch the house and the man went off on his business trip. When he returned, the two met up again.

'So,' said the man, 'did anything happen while I was out of town?'

The friend looked downcast. 'I'm afraid I've got bad news for you,' he said. 'Just a couple of hours after you left, I saw a strange car pull up outside your house. A man got out, rang the doorbell of your house and your wife greeted him with a passionate embrace and let him in. A few minutes later, the light went on in your bedroom and I saw them kissing. Then they drew the curtains.'

'Then what happened?'

'I don't know,' said the friend. 'I couldn't see.'

'You see what I mean? There's always that doubt.'

Why did the polygamist cross the aisle?
—To get to the other bride.

A man was sitting at the bar of his local tavern downing shots of whisky when one of his friends came in and spotted him.

'Joe,' said the friend. 'What are you doing? I've known you for over twenty years and I've never known you to drink. What's up?'

Knocking back another shot of whisky, Joe replied: 'My wife just ran off with my best friend.'

'But Joe,' protested the other man, 'I'm your best friend.'

Joe turned to him and said: 'Not anymore. He is!'

Convinced that his wife was having an affair, a husband decided to confront her.

'Is it my friend John?' he demanded.

'No.'

'Is it my friend Lou?'

'No.'

'Is it my friend Dave?'

'No,' she screamed. 'What is it with you – don't you think I have any friends of my own?'

Did you hear about the man who muttered a few words in church and found himself married? Ten months later, he muttered something in his sleep and found himself divorced.

During a heated argument, a husband said to his wife: 'Admit it, the only reason you married me was because my aunt left me two million pounds.'

'Don't be ridiculous,' the wife responded. 'I didn't care who left it to you.'

One night, a man went into a bar and asked the bartender for a drink. Then he asked for another. After a couple more drinks, the bartender was getting worried.

'What's the matter?' the bartender asked the man.

'My wife and I got into a fight,' explained the guy. 'And now she isn't talking to me for a whole thirty days.'

The bartender thought about this for a while. 'But, isn't it a good thing that she isn't talking to you?' asked the bartender.

The man replied: 'Yeah, except today is the last night.'

Why should a married man always forget his mistakes?
—Because there's no use in two people remembering the same thing.

Wife: Why don't you ever wear your wedding ring?
Husband: It cuts off my circulation.
Wife: It's meant to.

What do you call a woman who knows where her husband is every night?
—A widow.

A travelling salesman was testifying in divorce proceedings against his wife. His lawyer asked him what had made him suspect that his wife had been unfaithful.

The husband answered: 'Because I'm away all week, when I do get home I like to make it up to my wife. One Sunday morning we were in the middle of passionate love-making when the old lady in the apartment next door banged on the wall and shouted: 'Can't you at least stop all that at weekends?'

A young bride stepped out of the shower on her wedding night wrapped in a robe. Her husband said: 'There's no need to be shy now – we're married.'

So she removed her robe to reveal her naked body.

'You look great!' he purred. 'Can I take your picture?'

'Why?' asked the wife, embarrassed.

'So that I can be reminded of your beauty every minute of the day.'

He took the photo and then went to have a shower himself. Shortly afterwards he emerged wrapped in a robe.

'Why are you wearing a robe?' she asked. 'Remember there's no need to be shy now – we're married.'

So he took off his robe to reveal his naked body.

'Can I take your picture?' she asked.

'Why?' he asked with a knowing grin.

'So I can get it enlarged.'

A man approached a glamorous woman in a shopping mall. 'I seem to have lost my wife,' he said. 'Is it okay if I talk to you for a minute?'

'Sure,' replied the woman, 'but I don't see how that will help you find your wife.'

'Oh, it will,' he said. 'She always turns up the moment I start chatting to attractive women.'

While Rebecca lay on her deathbed, her husband Paul maintained a constant vigil by her side. As he held her fragile hand, his warm tears ran silently down his face, splashed on to hers and roused her from her slumber.

She looked up and her pale lips began to move slightly. 'My darling Paul,' she whispered.

'Ssshh!' he said tenderly. 'Don't wear yourself out by talking. Go back to sleep.'

But she was insistent. 'Paul,' she gasped, 'I must talk. There is something I must confess to you.'

'There's nothing to confess,' replied Paul between sobs. 'It's all right. Everything's all right now. Go to sleep.'

'No, my darling,' she persisted, 'I need to die in peace. I have to confess my sins. It pains me to say it but I had affairs with your best friend, your brother and your father.'

Paul mustered a pained smile and gently stroked her hand. 'Hush, my darling,' he said. 'Don't worry about it. I know all about the affairs. Why do you think I poisoned you?'

What's the difference between a marriage and a war?

—A marriage is a war where the enemies sleep together.

As they drove home from a party, a wife turned to her husband and said: 'Have I ever told you how sexy and irresistible to women you are?'

'I don't think you have,' he answered with a smirk.

'Then what the hell gave you that idea at the party?'

A wife said to her husband: 'Darling, let's go out tonight and have some fun.'

'Okay,' he said, 'but if you get home before I do, leave the hallway light on.'

A boy rushed home excitedly from school to tell his parents: 'I've got a part in the school play. I play a married man.'

'Well done, son,' said his father. 'Keep up the good work and one day you might get a speaking part.'

To mark their golden wedding anniversary, a couple were asked by a local newspaper reporter to reveal the secret of their long and happy marriage.

'Well,' explained the husband, 'it all dates back to our honeymoon. We visited the Grand Canyon and rode down to the bottom of the canyon by mule. We hadn't gone far when my wife's mule stumbled. My wife didn't do anything but just said quietly: "That's once." We carried on for a few hundred yards but then her mule stumbled again. "That's twice," she said softly. Then a few minutes later her mule stumbled for a third time. My wife calmly hopped down from the mule, produced a revolver from her purse and shot the animal dead. When I immediately protested about her treatment of the mule, she looked at me and said quietly: "That's once."'

A recently divorced man was in court to reach a settlement regarding his alimony payments. The judge said: 'After due consideration, I have decided to give your wife fifteen hundred pounds a month.'

'That's very generous of you, your honour,' said the man. 'And from time to time I'll try to send her a few quid myself.'

Two women friends were discussing their husbands. One said sadly: 'It seems like all Joe and I do is fight. I've been so upset lately that I've lost sixteen pounds.'

'Why don't you leave him?' asked her friend.

'Not yet. I want to lose another fourteen pounds first.'

On their first morning at home after returning from their honeymoon, the young bride said to her husband: 'If you make the toast and pour the juice, breakfast will be ready.'

'Great,' he said. 'What are we having?'

'Toast and juice.'

Mummy, Mummy...

'Are you sure this is how you learn to swim?'
—'Be quiet and get back in the sack!'

'Can I play in the sandbox?'
—'Not until I find a better place to bury Daddy.'

'Grandpa's going out!'
—'Well, throw on some more gasoline!'

'When will the paddling pool be full?'
—'Shut up and keep spitting!'

'Now that I'm sixteen can I start wearing lipstick and high heels?'
—'Don't be so silly, Gerald!'

'My teacher says I'm a vampire!'
—'Be quiet and drink your soup before it clots!'

'I've broken both my legs!'
—'Well, don't come running to me!'

'What's for dinner?'
—'Shut up and get back in the oven.'

'Why are we pushing the car off the cliff?'
—'Ssssh! You'll wake your father.'

'Can I lick the bowl?'
—'No, flush it like everyone else!'

'Why is Daddy running away?'
—'Hurry up and reload!'

Money

A man was walking through town one evening when a beggar in threadbare clothing approached him and asked him for five pounds.

'Why do you want the money?' asked the man. 'Is it to buy cigarettes?'

'No,' said the beggar.

'Is it to buy booze?'

'No.'

'Will you gamble it away?'

'No, I won't.'

'Then will you come home with me so that I can show my wife what happens to a guy who doesn't smoke, drink or gamble?'

A woman with a fifty pound note wedged in each ear went for a meeting with her bank manager.

'Mrs Jones is waiting outside,' the receptionist informed the manager.

'Ah yes, Mrs Jones,' he said, leafing through his files. 'She's a hundred pounds in arrears.'

A young man decided to buy his girlfriend some perfume for her birthday. He asked the shop assistant for some advice and she showed him a bottle of perfume costing fifty pounds.

'That's too expensive,' he said.

So she produced a smaller bottle, costing thirty pounds.

'That's still a bit expensive,' he said.

Becoming irritated, the assistant brought out a tiny fifteen-pound bottle.

'That's still too much,' he groaned. 'Can you show me something cheap?'

And so the assistant handed him a mirror.

Why is a tax loophole like a good parking spot?
—As soon as you see one, it's gone.

A man called on the vicar's wife, a woman well known for her charitable deeds.

'Madam,' he said, close to tears, 'I feel I must draw your attention to the awful plight of an impoverished family in this district. The father is dead, the mother is too ill to work and the nine children are starving. They are about to be turned out onto the cold and empty streets unless someone pays their rent, which amounts to six hundred pounds.'

'How terrible!' exclaimed the vicar's wife. 'May I ask who you are?'

The sympathetic visitor dabbed his handkerchief to his eyes. 'I'm the landlord.'

A banker fell overboard while piloting his riverboat. A man steering a boat travelling in the opposite direction immediately unhooked a lifebelt, held it up and, not knowing if the banker could swim, called out: 'Can you float alone?'

'Of course I can!' spluttered the banker. 'But this is a hell of a time to talk business!'

Every year Don entered the lottery at the state fair but because he had never won anything he decided to give up.

'Don't do that,' said his friend Mike. 'You never know, this could be your lucky year. You need to have faith. Look around and see if God sends you a message.'

So Don toured the fair looking for a sign but none was forthcoming until he noticed a large woman bending over next to her cake stand. As she did so, a huge gust of wind blew her dress over her head and a finger of fire wrote the number seven on each of her buttocks.

Interpreting this as divine inspiration, Don ran to the lottery booth and played the number 77. A few minutes later the winner was announced over the tannoy. It was 707.

A man was looking through the items for sale in the local newspaper. One read: 'Television for sale. £1 – Volume Stuck on Full.'

He thought to himself: 'I can't turn that down.'

INSURANCE AGENT TRANSLATIONS

He says: I'll look into that.
He means: I want to see if you've paid your last premium before I spend any more time with you.

He says: Why don't I call you back tomorrow?
He means: I'm playing golf this afternoon.

He says: I can't really refer you to another person.
He means: I hate anyone muscling in on my commission.

He says: That's quite an extensive list of losses.
He means: I think I'm going to throw up.

He says: Everything looks in order with your policy.
He means: Damn!

He says: If I don't call you back by next week, give me a call.
He means: I don't know what the hell to do. Maybe you will forget until the policy runs out.

He says: This may take a little time.
He means: Last week two of my clients moved into retirement homes.

He says: I'd like to check with my supervisor first.
He means: I can't figure out what's wrong with these numbers. Maybe the new kid with the degree knows what to do.

He says: I have some good news and some bad news.
He means: The good news is that I'm going to buy that new BMW. The bad news is that you're going to be paying for it.

A new patient was about to enter the hospital when she saw two white-coated doctors searching through the flower beds.

'Excuse me, have you lost something?' she asked.

'No,' replied one of the doctors. 'We're doing a heart transplant for a tax inspector and want to find a suitable stone!'

Four men were playing poker in the back room of a pub until one of the four, Ed, lost twelve hundred pounds on a single hand. The shock was so great that Ed immediately suffered a heart attack and dropped dead at the table. The others nominated Harry to break the sad news to Ed's widow but warned him to be discreet and not add to the woman's pain.

Arriving at Ed's house, Harry knocked on the door. Ed's wife answered and asked him what he wanted.

'Your husband just lost twelve hundred pounds playing cards,' said Harry.

'What!' exclaimed the wife. 'In that case I hope he drops dead!'

'Okay,' said Harry. 'I'll tell him.'

A stockbroker's secretary answered the phone. 'I'm sorry,' she said. 'Mr Smythson is on another line.'

The caller said: 'This is Jerry Wilson. I want to know if he's bullish or bearish right now.'

'He's talking to his wife,' said the secretary. 'Right now I'd say he was sheepish.'

A man was sitting at a bar drowning his sorrows.

'What's up?' asked the bartender.

'Three months ago my father died and left me £60,000,' said the man. 'Two months ago my mother died and left me £40,000. Then last month an uncle died and left me £20,000. But this month? Nothing.'

An old hobo walked into a bank and said to the female teller: 'I want to open a goddamn account – and I want to open it now.'

'Excuse me, sir,' said the teller. 'What did you say?'

'I said I want to open a goddamn account, so get off your fat ass and sort it.'

'I'm very sorry, sir,' said the teller, 'but I will not be spoken to like that. We do not tolerate that kind of language in this bank.'

With that she left her window and went to fetch the manager.

'What seems to be the problem here?' asked the manager.

'There's no goddamn problem,' said the hobo. 'I just won twenty million quid in the lottery and I want to open a goddamn account in this goddamn bank!'

'I see,' said the manager. 'And this bitch is giving you a hard time?'

A man went into a bank and asked the teller to check his balance. So the teller pushed him over.

Mothers-in-law

A man, his wife and his mother-in-law were watching TV one evening when she suddenly announced: 'I've decided that I want to be cremated.'

'Okay,' said the man. 'I'll get your coat.'

A police chief warned a new recruit: 'As an officer you'll have some tough decisions to make. For instance, what would you do if you had to arrest your wife's mother?'

The recruit replied: 'Call for back-up.'

A big game hunter went on safari with his wife and mother-in-law. One night, the couple awoke to find the mother had vanished. They went off in search of her and in a nearby clearing they came across a terrifying sight – the mother-in-law was cornered by a snarling lion.

'What are we going to do?' cried the wife.

'Nothing,' said the husband. 'The lion got himself into this mess, he can get himself out of it!'

Members of a Bible study group were discussing how they would choose to spend the last four weeks of their lives if they knew they were about to die.

One said: 'I would go out into the community and spread the word of God.'

'Admirable,' chorused the rest of the group.

Another said: 'I would work unpaid in a hospital to try and help comfort the sick.'

'That's a wonderful idea,' chorused the rest of the group.

Then a man at the back said: 'I would go to my mother-in-law's house for the four weeks.'

'Why would you do that?' asked the others.

'Because that will make it the longest four weeks of my life!'

Jim told his drinking buddy Harry: 'I took my dog to the vet today because it bit my mother-in-law.'

'Did you have it put to sleep?' asked Harry.

'No,' said Jim. 'I had its teeth sharpened.'

A married couple were involved in a terrible accident that left the wife's face severely burned. The doctor informed the husband that they couldn't graft any skin from her body because she was too thin. So the husband offered to donate some of his own skin but the doctor said the only skin that was suitable was on the husband's buttocks.

The husband and wife agreed not to tell anyone where the grafted skin came from and made the doctor agree to sign a confidentiality pact because it was such a delicate matter.

After the surgery was completed, everyone was amazed at how beautiful the wife looked. Her new facial skin made her appear younger than ever.

One day, she was alone with her husband when she was overcome with emotion at his sacrifice. 'Darling,' she said, 'I just want to thank you for what you did for me. How can I ever repay you?'

'Honey,' he smiled, 'I get all the thanks I need every time I see your mother kiss you on the cheek!'

The bane of George's life was his vindictive mother-in-law who, to his horror, lived with his family. Every morning, as he was about to leave for the office, the mother-in-law would sidle up to him and whisper: 'If you don't treat my daughter properly after I'm dead, I'll dig up from the grave and haunt you!'

It was the same whenever George came home for lunch. The mother-in-law would grab him and hiss: 'If you don't treat my daughter properly after I'm dead, I'll dig up from the grave and haunt you!'

Again at night, the vicious mother-in-law would collar him on the way to bed and growl: 'If you don't treat my daughter properly after I'm dead, I'll dig up from the grave and haunt you!'

He recounted his desperate life with his mother-in-law to a friend who, after not seeing George for six months, asked him how the old woman was feeling.

'She's not feeling anything,' said George. 'She died a month ago.'

'Aren't you worried about her sinister threat?' asked the friend.

'Not really,' said George, 'but just to be on the safe side, I buried her face down. Let her dig!'

What are the two worst things about a mother-in-law?
—Her faces.

A woman woke her husband in the middle of the night and said: 'I think there's a burglar downstairs and he's eating the cake that my mother made for us.'

'Who do you want me to phone?' said the husband. 'The police or an ambulance?'

A man was walking along the beach one day when he stumbled across a lamp. He rubbed it and a genie appeared.

The genie granted the man two wishes but told him that whatever he wished for, his mother-in-law would get double.

The man thought for a moment and said: 'First, give me a million pounds. Then beat me half to death.'

A young wife came home one day to find her mother standing in a bucket of water and her finger stuck in a light socket. The young husband was poised over the light switch.

'Isn't it wonderful, darling?' said the mother. 'Michael has come up with this wonderful idea for curing my rheumatism.'

Bill and Harry were walking down the street when Bill noticed six men kicking and punching his mother-in-law.

'Are you going to help?' asked Harry.

'No,' said Bill. 'Six should be enough.'

A lawyer informed his client: 'Your mother-in-law has passed away in her sleep. Shall we order burial, embalming or cremation?'

'Take no chances,' said the son-in-law. 'Order all three.'

A man said to his friend: 'My mother-in-law's an angel.'

'You're lucky,' said the friend. 'Mine's still alive.'

Music

Did you hear about the guy who thought Bob Marley and the Wailers were the sailors who caught Moby Dick?

How do you make Lady Gaga cry?
—Poker face.

What's the difference between an onion and an accordion?
—Nobody cries when you chop up an accordion.

Why do bagpipers walk when they play?
—To get away from the noise.

Why did the Boy Scout take up the banjo?
—They make good paddles.

A man went on holiday to a tropical island. As soon as he stepped off the plane, he heard the sound of drums playing. He went to the beach and he still heard the drums. While he was eating lunch, he heard the drums. That evening, he went to a barbecue and still he heard the drums. That night, when he tried to go to sleep, the drums were still playing.

This went on for several days and nights and eventually reached the point where the man couldn't sleep at night because of the drums. Finally, he went down to the hotel's reception and asked for the manager.

'Excuse me,' he said. 'What's with these drums? Don't they ever stop? I can't get any sleep.'

The manager said: 'No! Drums must never stop. It's very bad if drums stop.'

'Why?'

The hotel manager replied: 'When drums stop ... bass solo begins.'

There was a twenty pound note on the floor. Of a thrash guitarist, a drummer who keeps good time and a drummer who keeps bad time, who picked it up?
—The drummer who keeps bad time. The other drummer doesn't exist, and the thrash guitarist doesn't care about notes anyway.

What's the difference between a French horn section and a '57 Chevy?
—You can tune a '57 Chevy.

At a concert hall one night, the stage manager came across an oboe player and a viola player having a fight. He broke the fight up and asked what the problem was.

The oboe player said: 'He broke my reed! I was just about to play my big solo when he broke my reed!'

'Well?' said the stage manager to the viola player. 'What do you say to that?'

Annoyed, the viola player replied: 'He undid two of my strings but he won't tell me which ones!'

How many tenors does it take to change a light bulb?
—Six. One to do it, and five to say: 'It's too high for him.'

A ranch owner and a truck driver were on death row and were to be executed on the same day. The day came and they were taken to the gas chamber.

The warden asked the ranch owner if he had a last request, to which the cowboy replied: 'I sure do, warden. I'd be mighty grateful if you'd play "Achy Breaky Heart" for me before I have to go.'

'Sure, we can do that,' said the warden. He then turned to the truck driver. 'And what's your last request?' he asked.

The truck driver replied: 'Kill me first.'

A tourist was sightseeing in Vienna. She came upon the tomb of Ludwig van Beethoven and began reading the commemorative plaque, only to be distracted by a low scratching noise, as if something was rubbing against a piece of paper.

She walked over to a local person and asked what the scratching sound was. The local replied: 'Oh, that's Beethoven. He's decomposing.'

Little Davey was practising the violin in his bedroom while his father was trying to read in the living room. The family dog was lying on the living room floor and as the screeching sounds of little Davey's violin reached his ears, he began to howl loudly.

The father listened to the dog and the violin for as long as he could. Then he jumped up, slammed his paper to the floor and yelled above the noise: 'For pity's sake, can't you play something the dog doesn't know?'

A girl went out on a date with a trumpet player and when she came back her room mate asked her: 'Well, how was it? Did his embouchure make him a great kisser?'

'Not really,' the girl replied. 'That dry, tight, tiny little pucker; it was no fun at all.'

The next night she went out with a tuba player and when she came back her room mate asked: 'Well, how was his kissing?'

'Awful!' the girl exclaimed. 'Those huge, rubbery, blubbery, slobbering slabs of meat; oh, it was just horrible!'

The next night she went out with a French horn player and when she came back her room mate asked her: 'Well, how was his kissing?'

'Well,' the girl replied, 'his kissing was just so-so; but I loved the way he held me.'

What's the range of a tuba?
—About twenty yards, if you have a good arm.

A guitarist was on the phone to his agent. He felt concerned that he hadn't played any gigs for a while. His agent told him: 'Listen, there aren't any gigs out there, but I found you something. I got you a gig bagging lions.'

The guitarist was confused and asked: 'What does that have to do with my playing?'

His agent answered: 'Look, the gig pays two hundred bucks for each lion that you bag. Don't worry about playing.'

He thought for a moment about his dire financial situation and decided to accept the offer. Not wanting to miss any practice time, he took his guitar with him while looking for the lions. After a while he noticed a lion coming towards him and the only thing that he could think of doing was playing his guitar.

He started to play a beautiful ballad and then noticed that the lion was starting to doze off. When it fell asleep, he grabbed the lion, bagged it and threw it in the back of his truck. He went on a little further and saw another lion. Again, he played a beautiful ballad and again the lion fell asleep. This continued all afternoon and by early evening the guitarist had around fifty lions in his truck.

Just as he was thinking of finishing for the day, he saw another lion. He thought: 'What the heck, one more won't hurt.' He started to play his ballad and noticed that the lion was not getting sleepy, so he started to play louder. The lion began to run towards the guitarist, so he started to play faster and faster but the lion kept coming towards him. Finally the lion jumped on the guitar player and ate him.

On the truck one lion turned to another and said: 'I told you that when he got to the deaf one, the gig would be over.'

What do you call someone who hangs around with musicians?
—A drummer.

What's the last thing a drummer says in a band?
—Hey, guys, why don't we try one of my songs?

How can you tell when a drummer's at the door?
—He doesn't know when to come in.

How is a drum solo like a sneeze?
—You can tell when it's coming but you can't do anything about it.

What's the best way to confuse a drummer?
—Put a sheet of music in front of him.

How can you tell when a drummer is walking behind you?
—You can hear his knuckles dragging on the ground.

What do you call a drummer who breaks up with his girlfriend?
—Homeless.

What is Eminem's favourite paper?
—Rapping paper

Old People

An old man visited the doctor and after an extensive medical examination, the doctor said: 'I have good news and bad news for you. Do you want the good news or the bad news first?'

The old man was concerned and asked for the bad news first.

The doctor said: 'I'm sorry to say that you have cancer and you have only about two years to live.'

The old man was shocked. 'So what's the good news?' he asked.

The doctor said: 'You also have Alzheimer's and in approximately three months you will have forgotten everything I have told you.'

A woman bumped into an elderly neighbour one morning. The neighbour only had one arm.

'Where are you off to, Tom?' she asked.

'To change a light bulb,' he answered.

'Oh,' she said. 'That will be a bit awkward, won't it?'

'Not really,' he said. 'I've still got the receipt.'

An old woman went to a gynaecologist for the first time. He was young and thorough and the old woman was naturally embarrassed throughout the examination. Finally, he told her to get dressed and to come into his office so that they could talk about his findings.

The old woman listened intently as the doctor gave her the results. She then said she had just one question for him.

'What's that?' asked the gynaecologist.

'Tell me, young man, does your mother know what you do for a living?'

Old academics never die, they just lose their faculties.

Old accountants never die, they just lose their balance.

Old actors never die, they just drop a part.

Old anthropologists never die, they just become history.

Old architects never die, they just lose their structures.

Old astronauts never die, they just go to another world.

An elderly widow and widower were dating for about three years when the man finally asked her to marry him and she immediately said, 'Yes'. The next morning the widower couldn't remember the widow's answer to his marriage proposal. He thought long and hard and tried to visualize her reaction. Was she happy or was she annoyed? Unable to remember, he eventually decided to phone her and embarrassingly admitted that he couldn't remember whether she had said 'yes' or 'no'.

'I'm so glad you called,' she said. 'I remember saying "yes" to someone but I couldn't remember who it was.'

After attending church for most of her life, a 103-year-old lady suddenly stopped going. When the minister met her in the street one day, he asked her why she was no longer a regular member of the congregation. She leaned towards him and whispered: 'When I reached ninety years of age, I expected to be taken by God at any time. Then I got to ninety-five, then one hundred and now I am one hundred and three. So I thought that God must be very busy and has forgotten about me and I don't really want to remind Him.'

Old bankers never die, they just lose interest.

Old baseball players never die, they just run their last lap.

Old basketball players never die, they just go on dribbling.

Old beekeepers never die, they just buzz off.

Old bookkeepers never die, they just lose their figures.

Old bureaucrats never die, they just waste away.

Two police officers saw an old woman staggering along the street. They stopped their patrol car and told her that she had had too much to drink. Instead of taking her to jail they decided to take her home. They loaded her into the police car with one officer driving and the other sitting in the back seat with the drunken woman. They drove around the streets and kept asking her where she lived but all she would say was 'You're passionate', while stroking the officer's arm.

After getting the same response, 'You're passionate,' for the umpteenth time, they stopped the car and said to the old woman: 'Look, we have been driving around this city for over two hours and still you haven't told us where you live.'

The old woman replied: 'I keep trying to tell you, you're passing it!'

Two gas company engineers were making house calls when the younger man decided to 'wind-up' his older colleague about his age. 'My God, you're looking worn out today!'

'Oh yeah?' replied the older guy. 'I may be older than you but I bet I am fitter and can outrun you.'

'Okay, you're on,' said the younger guy. 'Let's have a race around the block.'

So they both sprinted around the block but were overtaken by an elderly lady.

'What are you doing?' they panted.

The old lady replied: 'Well, you've just been at my home checking my gas boiler. So when I saw you both run away, I figured I'd better run too!'

An elderly man boasted to a group of teenagers about his level of fitness. 'I can do fifty sit-ups, fifty push-ups and walk five miles every single day. I'm as fit as a fiddle. Do you boys want to know why? I don't smoke, I don't drink, I don't stay up late and I have never chased after women. And tomorrow I'm going to be celebrating my eighty-fifth birthday.'

'Oh really?' said one of the teenagers. 'How?'

Old cashiers never die, they just check out.

Old chauffeurs never die, they just lose their drive.

Old chemists never die, they just fail to react.

Old cleaners never die, they just kick the bucket.

Old computer technicians never die, they just lose their memory.

An old man attended a school reunion but was dismayed when his surviving classmates began discussing their ill-health and various ailments – heart problems, kidney stones and liver complaints. When he returned home, his wife asked if he had enjoyed his evening.

'No! It wasn't much of a reunion, more like an organ recital!'

Three old men went out for a walk. The first old man remarked: 'It's windy, isn't it?'

The second old man replied: 'No, it's Thursday.'

The third old man chimed in: 'So am I, let's go for a beer!'

An old man went to the movies for the first time in many years. He travelled from his small rural town to the big city. After buying his ticket he went to buy some popcorn. Handing the attendant two dollars, he couldn't help but remark that the last time he visited the movies popcorn was only ten cents.

The attendant smiled: 'Well, sir, you're really going to enjoy the movie. We have sound now!'

A distinguished elderly gentleman was taking a walk in the park one day in the hope of finding companionship following the recent death of his beloved wife. He noticed an attractive grey-haired lady sitting on a bench and politely asked: 'May I sit down next to you?'

The lady smiled at the smartly dressed man and replied: 'Of course.' They got into conversation and chatted for over two hours about their interests – movies, music, food – and found they shared the same taste in all of them. They even discovered that they originally hailed from the same part of the country and that they had both been recently bereaved after long and happy marriages. Just before the time came for them to part, the elderly man asked the lady if he could ask her two questions.

'Certainly,' she said.

The man took out his handkerchief, spread it on the ground and knelt down on one knee. He took the lady's hand in his and, looking lovingly into her eyes, said: 'Alice, we have so much in common and I feel that we have known each other all our lives even though we have actually known each other only a few hours. Would you do me the honour of being my wife?'

'Yes,' she replied, and kissed him gently on the cheek before adding: 'You said you were going to ask two questions. What is the second? '

The elderly man said: 'Will you help me up?'

The proprietor of a general store hired a young female assistant who wore very short skirts to work. One day a young man came into the shop and asked for some raisin bread. Since the raisin bread was located on the top shelf, she had to climb a stepladder to reach it, in the process giving him the chance to look up her skirt. He enjoyed the view so much that when she came down, he suddenly remembered he needed more raisin bread – just as an excuse to get her to climb the ladder again.

By now the other male customers in the store had realized what was going on and they, too, took turns to ask for raisin bread. Each time the girl climbed the ladder to fetch the raisin bread, and each time they got to see up her skirt. After her seventh climb, she was beginning to feel exhausted. From the top step, she looked down at the group of men and spotted an old timer, who had yet to be served, gazing up at her. In a bid to save herself another trip, she asked him: 'Is yours raisin, too?'

'No,' replied the old man, 'but it's starting to twitch!'

Old dancers never die, they just step away.

Old doctors never die, they just lose patience.

Old electricians never die, they just lose contact.

Old engineers never die, they just lose their bearings.

Old environmentalists never die, they are just recycled.

An old man became increasingly hard of hearing over many years. Eventually, he went to the doctor to be fitted with a hearing aid that gave him one hundred per cent hearing.

After a month he went back to the doctor for his check-up and the doctor said: 'Your hearing is perfect. Your family must be really pleased that you can hear again?'

'Oh, I haven't told my family yet,' said the old man. 'I just sit around listening to their conversations. I've changed my will three times, so far!'

An old man was running a fairground tent and proclaimed: 'For sixty pounds I'll teach you to be a mind reader.' A passing teenager was intrigued by this offer and, hoping to learn a new skill, he approached the tent.

'Right,' said the old man, handing the teenager a garden hose. 'I want you to hold this and look in the end.'

'What for?' asked the teenager.

'It's all part of becoming a mind reader,' said the old man.

So the teenager reluctantly looked in the end of the hose and saw only darkness. Suddenly the old man turned on the tap and water gushed out of the hose and drenched the teenager.

'I knew you were going to do something like that!' yelled the teenager.

'That'll be sixty pounds then,' said the old man.

An old man retired and bought a modest home near a school. His first few weeks of retirement in his new home were spent in peace and tranquillity. Then the new school year started and on the first afternoon three boys, full of youthful after-school exuberance, went down the street beating every rubbish bin they encountered. This crashing percussion continued day after day until the old man decided to take action.

The following afternoon he went out to meet the three young percussionists as they merrily crashed and banged their way down the street. Stopping them, he said: 'I can see you boys are having a lot of fun playing the rubbish bins and I enjoy hearing you expressing your exuberance this way. In fact, I did much the same thing myself when I was your age. Will you do me a favour? I'll give each of you boys one pound if you'll promise to come around every day and do your thing.' The three boys were elated with this deal and continued to crash the rubbish bins each day.

After a few days the old man greeted the boys again but this time he was wearing a sad smile. 'This recession has really dented my income,' he sighed, 'and I'm only able to pay you fifty pence each to beat the bins.' The boys were obviously not happy but accepted the old man's offer and continued making their noise.

A few days later, the old man approached the boys as they made their noisy way down the street. 'I haven't had my pension yet,' he said apologetically, 'so I can't give you more than twenty-five pence each. Is that okay?'

'A lousy twenty-five pence?' said the leader. 'If you think we are going to waste our time beating these bins for that, you're nuts! No way, mister, we quit!'

And the old man enjoyed peace and quiet from then on.

Old farmers never die, they just go to seed.

Old foresters never die, they just pine away.

Old garage men never die, they just retire.

Old golfers never die, they just lose their drive.

An old chicken farmer walked up to the ticket window at the movie theatre and the ticket agent asked: 'Sir, what's that on your shoulder?'

The farmer said: 'That's my pet rooster, Chuck. Wherever I go, Chuck goes.'

'I'm sorry, sir,' said the ticket agent. 'We can't allow animals in the theatre.'

Refusing to be dictated to, the wily farmer went round the corner, stuffed the bird down his overalls, returned to the booth, bought a ticket and entered the theatre, where he sat down next to two old widows named Mildred and Marge.

The movie started and the rooster began to squirm. The old farmer unbuttoned his fly so Chuck could stick his head out and watch the movie.

'Marge,' whispered Mildred.

'What?' said Marge.

I think the guy next to me is a pervert.'

'What makes you think that?' asked Marge.

'He undid his pants and he has his thing out,' whispered Mildred.

'Well, don't worry about it,' said Marge. 'Hell, at our age, we've seen 'em all.'

'I thought so too,' said Mildred. 'But this one's eating my popcorn.'

Three old ladies were discussing the problems of ageing. One said: 'I sometimes find myself standing at the refrigerator with a block of cheese in my hand and I can't remember whether I need to put it away or make myself a sandwich.'

The second said: 'Sometimes I find myself on the upstairs landing and can't remember whether I'm on my way up or on my way down.'

'I'm glad I don't have that problem – touch wood,' said the third, rapping her knuckles on the table. She then paused for a second and said: 'That must be the door, I'll get it.'

An old married couple were discussing their future plans. The husband asked his wife: 'If I die before you, what will you do?'

After some thought, she replied: 'Well, I will probably look to share a house with three other single or widowed women and, as I'm still active for my age, I'll look for roommates who are slightly younger than me. What about you? What will you do if I die first?'

'Probably the same,' he replied.

An old man went to the doctor for his annual check-up. After the examination, the doctor explained that the man had a serious heart murmur. 'Do you smoke?' asked the doctor.

'No,' replied the old man.

'Do you drink to excess?'

'No.'

'Do you still have a sex life.'

'Yes, I do,' said the old man.

'Well, with your serious heart condition you had better give up half your sex life.'

'Which half?' asked the old man. 'The looking or the thinking?'

A young man asked a rich old man how he had made his money. The old man sat the young man down and said: 'Well, son, it was 1932 in the depth of the Great Depression. Times were hard and I was down to my last nickel. I invested that nickel in an apple. I spent the entire day polishing that apple and then sold it for ten cents. The next day I invested the ten cents in two apples. I spent the entire day polishing those two apples and at the end of the day I sold them for twenty cents. I continued this system for one month, by the end of which I had accumulated $2.50. Then the wife's father died and left us two million dollars.'

Two old men, one a retired history professor and the other a retired professor of psychology, were taking a vacation in Italy with their wives. Sitting out on the villa balcony watching the sunset, the history professor asked the psychology professor: 'Have you read Marx?'

To which the professor of psychology replied: 'Yes, I think it's these wicker chairs.'

Old lawyers never die, they just lose their appeal.

Old magicians never die, they just disappear.

Old mathematicians never die, they just go off on a tangent.

Two old married women were discussing their husbands over coffee one day. One said: 'Oh, I do wish Harry would stop biting his nails. It's a horrible habit.'

Her friend replied, 'My Bert used to do that until I cured him of it.'

'How did you do that?' asked the first woman.

'I hid his teeth!'

Old pacifists never die, they just go to peaces.

Old photographers never die, they just stop developing.

Old pilots never die, they just go to a higher plane.

Old plumbers never die, they just go down the drain.

Old policemen never die, they just cop out.

Old postal carriers never die, they just lose their zip.

Old investors never die, they just roll over.

A retired schoolteacher approached a young man in a Post Office. He asked the young man if he would address a postcard for him as the arthritis in his hands was playing him up.

'Certainly,' said the young man.

'Now would you be so kind as to write a short note on the postcard and sign it for me?' asked the retired schoolteacher.

'No problem,' said the young man. So the young man wrote out the postcard following the older man's dictation.

'Is there anything else I can do for you?' asked the young man.

'Yes,' replied the retired schoolteacher. 'Can you write at the bottom of the postcard, "P.S. please excuse the sloppy handwriting!"'

Old quilters never die, they just go under cover.

Old sculptors never die, they just lose their marbles.

Old seers never die, they just lose their vision.

Old shoemakers never die, they just lose their soles.

Three old men were discussing their lives.

One said: 'I'm still a once-a-night man.'

The second said: 'I'm a twice-a-night man.'

The third said: 'My wife will tell you that I'm a five-times-a-night man. You know, I really shouldn't drink so much tea before I go to bed.'

Two elderly ladies were driving along in a motor car so large they could hardly see over the dashboard. They were cruising along when they came to an intersection. The lights were showing red yet they went straight across the intersection. The passenger was somewhat surprised but thought she must have been mistaken about the red light. Further on, they came to another intersection and the light was red. Again they went straight through and the passenger was certain they had gone through a red light this time. A few miles further on they came to yet another intersection and the light was red. Yet again they went through a red light. The passenger was concerned for their safety so she decided to say something.

'Hey, Mildred,' she said. 'That's the third red light you have driven through; you're going to get us killed.'

'Oh dear,' replied Mildred. 'Am I driving?'

An elderly couple went out to celebrate their fiftieth wedding anniversary. At the end of the evening the man had a tear in his eye. His wife looked lovingly at him and asked if he was being sentimental, thinking about their fifty wonderful years together.

'No,' he replied. 'I was thinking about when we first met and your father threatened me with a shotgun and said that he would have me thrown in jail for fifty years if I didn't marry you. Tomorrow I'd be a free man!'

Old tanners never die, they just go into hiding.

Old teachers never die, they just lose their class.

Old vampires never die, they just ... don't.

The family of an increasingly frail old man decided that they couldn't care for him properly at home and that he would be better off in a nursing home. The old man wasn't happy but was soon convinced by his family that this was for the best so he went along with their decision.

On his first day in the nursing home he lay in his

bed feeling miserable, lonely and abandoned. Some time later an orderly called in to check on him. She noticed he was looking dejected so she decided to stay a while and chat with him. 'How are you doing?' she asked him.

The elderly man just grunted at her.

'This your first day?' she persisted.

The old man nodded his head.

Eventually, the orderly managed to engage the old man in conversation and they chatted, during which time she noticed the old man's room was filled with flowers, cards and balloons from his family and friends. On a table she noticed a large bowl of peanuts and, while they were talking, she kept helping herself to handfuls of the peanuts. After two hours, the orderly said she must get on and see to the other patients. The old man thanked her for spending time with him and said that he was feeling much better now.

Before leaving, the orderly said that she, too, had enjoyed their chat. 'But I feel awful as I've eaten most of your peanuts. I hope you don't mind?'

'That's alright,' he replied. 'My family keep buying them for me but since I have had these false teeth I can only suck the chocolate off them!'

Old watchmakers never die, they just run out of time.

Old weathermen never die, they reign forever.

Old wrestlers never die, they just lose their grip.

Old yachtsmen never die, they just keel over.

A retiring farmer needed to dispose of his animals and decided to give a horse to the homes where the man was boss and a chicken to the homes where the woman was boss. Calling at a house at the end of the lane he asked: 'Who's the boss around here?'

'I am,' said the man.

The farmer asked him whether he'd prefer a black horse or a brown horse.

'A black horse,' replied the man.

'No, a brown horse would be better,' said his wife.

'I'd really prefer a black horse,' said the man.

'No, we'll have the brown one,' insisted his wife.

So the farmer gave them a chicken!

Politicians

Canvassing for the election, a US politician visited an Indian reservation in an attempt to pick up some votes. He stood on a wooden box and made an impassioned speech.

First, he promised better health care on the reservations, an announcement that was greeted by his audience with cries of 'Kaya! Kaya!'

Delighted with the response, he then promised significant tax cuts and again the Indians responded with shouts of 'Kaya! Kaya!'

'I've got them eating out of my hand,' he thought to himself. 'This is amazing!'

In conclusion he promised to return sixty per cent

of the land that had been taken from the Indians by previous generations. The crowd yelled back: 'Kaya! Kaya!'

He stepped down from his box and was so encouraged by the audience reaction that he asked the chief if he could deliver another speech the following week.

'We'll discuss it on the way back to your car,' said the chief, who proceeded to escort the politician to his limo parked next to a cattle pen.

'They really liked what I had to say,' said the politician.

'You think so?' replied the chief. 'Hey, watch your shoes! You almost stepped in that big pile of kaya.'

After getting a haircut, a church minister asked a barber how much he owed him. 'There is no charge,' said the barber. 'I consider it a service to the Lord.' The next morning when the barber arrived at his shop, he found twelve Bibles and a thank you note from the minister at the front door.

Later that day a police officer got his hair cut at the same shop. He then asked how much it was. 'No charge,' said the barber. 'I consider it a service to the community.' The next morning when the barber arrived at his hop, he found twelve doughnuts and a thank you note from the police officer at the front door.

That afternoon a politician got his hair cut at the same barber's. Afterwards he asked how much it was. 'No charge,' said the barber. 'I consider it a service to the country.' The next morning when the barber arrived at his shop, he found twelve politicians at the front door.

A cannibal went shopping at a newly opened cannibal supermarket, where ordinary people cost twenty pounds a head but politicians cost fifty pounds.

The cannibal asked: 'Why do politicians cost so much?'

The checkout girl said: 'Do you know how tough it is to clean one of those?'

What do you have if three politicians are buried up to their necks in sand?
—Not enough sand.

How do you stop a politician from drowning?
—You take your foot off his head.

A young man in his early twenties was still living with his parents but seemed to have no idea about a future career. In the hope of determining what he might be best suited to, they set up a secret test. Placing a ten pound note, a Bible and a bottle of whisky on the hall table, they then hid from view in a nearby cupboard. The father explained to his wife: 'If our son takes the money, he will be a businessman; if he takes the Bible, he will be a man of the cloth but if he takes the bottle of whisky, I fear he will end up a drunkard.'

Peering through a crack in the door, they saw their son inspect the items on the table. First, he picked up the ten pound note, held it up to the light and slipped it into his pocket. Then he picked up the Bible, flicked through the pages, and put it in another pocket. Finally he snatched the bottle of whisky, took a swig, and carried all three items off to his room.

'Damn!' groaned the watching father. 'Our son is going to be a politician!'

Two politicians were waiting in line at the bank when a gang of armed robbers burst in. While some of the robbers vaulted the counter, the rest made the customers line up before snatching their money and jewellery.

Moments before the gang reached the politicians,

one politician pressed a wad of cash into the other's hand and said: 'Here's that hundred pounds I owe you.'

How can you tell when a politician is lying?
—His lips are moving.

A lifelong Republican supporter announced on his deathbed that he was switching his allegiance to the Democrats.

'What the hell are you thinking?' said a friend. 'You've always been a rabid Republican. Why do you now suddenly want to become a Democrat?'

'Because I'd rather it was one of them that died than one of us.'

Psychiatrists

A man told his psychiatrist: 'I can't stop deep-frying all my belongings in batter. I've deep-fried my mobile phone, I've deep-fried my laptop, I've deep-fried my DVD player and I've even battered my jeans. What's wrong with me?'

The psychiatrist took a deep breath and replied: 'It appears to me that you're frittering your life away!'

As his new patient relaxed on the couch, a psychiatrist said to him: 'Since this is your first session with me, perhaps you should start at the very beginning.'

'Certainly,' replied the patient. 'In the beginning, I created the heavens and the earth ...'

Four psychiatrists attending a convention got chatting in the bar one evening. One said: 'People are always coming to us with their guilt and fears but we have no one to whom we can go with our problems.'

The other three nodded in agreement.

'Since we are all professionals,' said the first, 'why don't we take some time right now to hear each other out?'

The other three agreed.

The first then confessed: 'I have an uncontrollable urge to kill all my patients.'

The second said: 'Because I love expensive clothes and fast cars I find ways to cheat my patients out of their money whenever possible so that I can buy the things that I want.'

The third said: 'I've got a real bad drug addiction and I often buy stuff from my patients.'

The fourth psychiatrist said: 'I know it's wrong, but no matter how hard I try, I just can't keep a secret ...'

Psychiatrists say that one in four people are mentally ill. Check three of your friends. If they are okay, you're the one!

A man visited a psychiatrist and listed all the things that were wrong with his life. 'I've got no job, no money and no love life,' he said dejectedly.

After listening to his patient's story, the psychiatrist said: 'I think your problem is low self-esteem. It's very common among losers!'

A psychiatrist met a fellow psychiatrist on the street. 'You're fine,' he said. 'How am I?'

A man went to a psychiatrist. 'Doctor,' he said, 'whenever I get into bed, I think there's someone hiding under it. It's driving me crazy. I haven't slept at night for months.'

'I see,' said the psychiatrist. 'I think I can cure you but it will require at least six months of weekly sessions and I charge a hundred pounds per session.'

The man said he would think about it and left.

A month later, the two men bumped into each other in the street. 'Why didn't you come to see me again?' asked the psychiatrist.

'You were too expensive,' replied the man, 'and anyway a bartender cured me for five pounds.'

'How did he manage that?' demanded the psychiatrist.

'He told me to cut the legs off the bed.'

How do you spot a psychiatrist in a nudist colony?
—He's the one listening instead of looking.

A psychiatrist is a person who gives you expensive answers that your wife will give you for free.

A psychiatrist was showing a male patient a series of ink blots. 'What do you think this is?' asked the psychiatrist.

'It's a naked lady in the shower,' replied the patient.

'And this one?'

'A topless woman on the beach.'

'And this?'

'A couple making love.'

'I'm sorry,' said the psychiatrist, 'but you're a sex maniac.'

'What do you mean?' said the patient. 'You're the one showing me dirty pictures.'

What did the Freudian analyst say to his patient? —'If it isn't one thing, it's your mother.'

A man went to a psychiatrist and said: 'You must help me. My wife is unfaithful to me. Every Saturday night she goes to Danny's Bar and picks up men. She sleeps with any guy who asks her. What can I do?'

'Okay,' said the psychiatrist. 'Just take a deep breath and relax. Now, tell me, where exactly is Danny's Bar?'

A mother was so worried about her unruly son that she became a bag of nerves and was unable to sleep at night. Increasingly concerned about the effect his wayward behaviour was having on her, she went to see a psychiatrist.

The psychiatrist told the mother: 'Constantly worrying about your son's behaviour is making you ill. I'm going to put you on a course of tranquilizers. Come and see me again in three months.'

On her return visit, the psychiatrist asked: 'Have the tranquilizers calmed you down?'

'Oh, yes. They are wonderful,' she said.

'And how is your son now?' asked the psychiatrist.

'Who cares?'

Religion

A minister was concerned about how to raise the two thousand pounds still needed to repair the church roof. Before Sunday service, he asked the organist to play some inspirational music to get the congregation into a giving mood.

'But I'm afraid I haven't any bright ideas as to what precisely you could play,' said the minister.

'Don't worry,' said the organist. 'I'll think of something.'

During the service, the minister made an appeal from the pulpit. 'As you know, we have so far raised eight thousand pounds to repair the church roof. But we still need another two. Many of you have already made generous donations but if you were able to dig just a little deeper into your pockets, it would mean so much to the community. So, if any of you can pledge another hundred pounds, perhaps you would be so kind as to stand up.'

At that point the organist started playing the National Anthem.

One day a Catholic, a Baptist and a Methodist were going fishing. No sooner had they set up their rods and nets in the middle of the lake than the Catholic remembered that he had left the food provisions on the shore. So he got out of the boat, walked on the water, picked up his supplies, walked back on the water and climbed into the boat.

Then the Baptist realized that they did not have enough bait. So he got out of the boat, walked on the water, bought a packet of bait, walked back on the water and climbed into the boat.

Then the Methodist, realizing that his watch wasn't working, wanted to buy a new one. So he took it off, got out of the boat ... but sunk all the way to the bottom of the lake.

The Catholic turned to the Baptist and said: 'I guess we should have told him where the rocks are!'

A Sunday school teacher asked her class why Joseph and Mary took Jesus with them to Jerusalem. A little girl answered: 'Because they couldn't get a babysitter.'

Three ministers were discussing the problems with cockroaches in their respective churches. The first said: 'I've tried putting down poison but nothing seems to get rid of them.'

The second said: 'I called in the council exterminator but even he couldn't destroy them.'

The third said: 'I managed to get rid of all mine. I simply baptized them all and I haven't seen them since!'

One day in Sunday school, the teacher was talking to the children about Jesus. 'Tim, where is Jesus?' asked the teacher.

'Jesus is in heaven,' answered Tim.

'Very good,' said the teacher.

The teacher then asked a little girl: 'Where is Jesus, Sophie?'

'Jesus is in my heart,' said Sophie sweetly.

The teacher smiled at Sophie and said: 'That's very nice.'

The teacher then asked Thomas: 'Where is Jesus?'

'Jesus is in my bathroom,' replied Thomas confidently.

'How do you mean?' asked the teacher, puzzled.

'Well, every morning my dad gets up, bangs on the bathroom door and yells: "Jesus Christ, are you still in there?"'

A preacher was told by his doctor that he had only a few weeks left to live.

He went home feeling very sad and when his wife heard the sad news, she said to him: 'Honey, if there's anything I can do to make you happy, tell me.'

The preacher answered: 'You know, dear, there's that box in the kitchen cabinet with what you always called your little secret in it and you said you never would want me to open it as long as you lived? Now that I'm about to go home to be with the Lord, why don't you show me what's in that secret box of yours?'

The preacher's wife hesitated for a moment but then decided to comply with her husband's wish. She got out the box and opened the lid. It contained three eggs and one hundred thousand pounds.

'What are those eggs doing in the box?' the preacher asked.

'Well, honey,' she replied, 'every time your sermon was really bad I put an egg in the box.'

Now the preacher had been preaching for more than forty years and, seeing only three eggs in that old shoe box, he started to feel very proud about himself and it warmed his soul.

'And what about the one hundred thousand pounds?' he asked.

'Oh, you see,' his wife whispered softly, 'every time there were a dozen eggs in the box, I sold them.'

Various religious leaders attended a conference in an attempt to answer the vexing question: 'Where does life begin?'

'At conception,' said the Catholic firmly.

'No, at birth,' said the Presbyterian.

'It's in between,' stated the Baptist. 'Life begins at twelve weeks when the foetus develops a functional heartbeat.'

'I disagree with all of you,' said the rabbi. 'Life begins when your last child leaves home and takes the dog with him.'

A vicar, notorious for his lengthy sermons, watched as a man got up and left halfway through his message. The same man returned before the end.

Afterwards, the vicar asked where he had gone.

'I went to get a haircut,' said the man.

'Why didn't you do that before the service?' asked the vicar.

The man replied: 'I didn't need one then!'

Three women were talking about the declining numbers in church attendance.

One said: 'The congregation at my church is down to about fifty.'

The second said: 'You're lucky. Most Sundays we consider ourselves fortunate if there are more than twenty people in the congregation at our church.'

The third woman said: 'That's nothing. It is so bad in our church that when the minister says "dearly beloved," I blush!'

A Sunday school teacher was struggling to open the four-digit combination lock on the church cabinet. She had been told the combination but couldn't remember it. In the end, she asked the vicar for help. After the first three numbers, the vicar paused, stared blankly for a moment and then looked heavenward as if for divine inspiration. Immediately he came up with the fourth number and opened the cabinet.

The teacher gushed: 'I'm so impressed by your faith.'

The vicar said: 'It's nothing really. You see, I can never remember the combination either. That's why I wrote the number on a piece of paper and stuck it to the ceiling.'

A pastor shocked his congregation when he announced that he was resigning from the church and moving to Spain.

After the service, a distraught woman came up to him and wailed: 'Oh, pastor, we are going to miss you. We really don't want you to leave.'

The pastor patted her hand reassuringly and said: 'It's very kind of you to say that but you never know, the next pastor might be even better than me.'

'Yes,' she sighed, her voice tinged with disappointment. 'That's what they said the last time too ... '

An Alabama preacher said to his congregation: 'Someone in this congregation has spread a rumour that I belong to the Ku Klux Klan. This is a horrible lie and one which a Christian community cannot tolerate. I am embarrassed and do not intend to accept this. Now, I want the party who did this to stand and ask forgiveness from God and this Christian Family.'

No one moved.

The preacher continued: 'Do you have the nerve to face me and admit this is a falsehood? Remember, you will be forgiven and in your heart you will feel glory. Now stand and confess your transgression.'

Again all was quiet.

Then slowly, a gorgeous woman with a body that would stop traffic rose from the third pew. Her head was bowed and her voice quivered as she spoke.

'Reverend, there has been a terrible mis-understanding. I never said you were a member of the Ku Klux Klan. I simply told a couple of my friends that you were a wizard under the sheets.'

Having invited some friends round to dinner, a couple asked their young son to say grace. The little boy was reluctant. 'But I wouldn't know what to say,' he protested.

'Just say what you've heard your father say,' advised his mother.

So the boy bowed his head and began: 'Dear Lord. Why the hell did we invite these people round when there's a match on television?'

A Christian fundamentalist couple felt it important to own a pet with similar leanings, so they visited a kennels that specialized in Christian fundamentalist dogs. One particular dog caught their eye. When they asked the dog to fetch the Bible, he did it immediately. When they instructed him to look up Psalm 23, he used his paws with great dexterity to locate the exact page.

They were so impressed that they bought the dog and took him home.

That night they had friends over and took the opportunity to show off their new fundamentalist dog. The friends were equally impressed and asked whether the dog could perform any of the usual doggie tricks as well. This momentarily stumped the couple who had not given any thought to ordinary dog tricks.

'We don't really know,' they said. 'We've only seen him perform religious tricks. I suppose there's one way to find out. Let's give it a try.'

So they called the dog and clearly pronounced the command 'Heel!'

The dog immediately jumped up, put his paw on the man's forehead, closed his eyes in concentration and bowed his head.

Nine-year-old Joey was asked by his mother what he had learned in Sunday school. Joey said: 'Well, Mum, our teacher told us how God sent Moses behind enemy lines on a rescue mission to lead the Israelites out of Egypt. When he got to the Red Sea, he had his engineers build a pontoon bridge and all the people walked across safely. Then he used his walkie-talkie to radio headquarters and call in an air strike. They sent in bombers to blow up the bridge and all the Israelites were saved.'

'Now, Joey, is that really what your teacher taught you?' his mother asked.

Joey replied: 'Well, no, Mum, but if I told it the way the teacher did, you'd never believe it.'

One afternoon a new vicar was doing his rounds of meeting his parishioners. All went well until he came to a cottage on the outskirts of a village.

Someone was obviously at home but even though the vicar knocked on the door several times, nobody answered. Finally he took out his card and wrote on the back: 'Revelation 3:20.'

The next day as he was counting the collection, the vicar noticed that his card had been left in the plate. Below his message was written: 'Genesis 3:10.'

Revelation 3:20 reads: 'Behold, I stand at the door and knock. If any man hears my voice, and opens the door, I will come in to his house and eat with him, and he will eat with me.' Genesis 3:10 reads: 'And he answered, I heard you in the garden; I was afraid and hid from you because I was naked.'

A clergyman was walking down the street when he came upon a group of young boys who were crowded around a dog. Concerned that the boys might be mistreating the animal, he went over and asked them what they were doing.

One of the boys replied: 'The dog is an old neighbourhood stray. We take him home with us sometimes but since only one of us can take him, we're having a contest: whichever one of us tells the biggest lie can take him home today.'

The clergyman was horrified. 'You boys shouldn't be having a contest about telling lies! Don't you know it's a sin to lie?' He then launched into a ten-minute sermon against lying, concluding with the words: 'Why, when I was your age, I never told a lie.'

Stunned into silence, the boys lowered their heads. Just as the clergyman thought he had got through to them, the smallest boy gave a deep sigh and handed him the leash: 'All right, Reverend,' he said. 'You win. You can take him home.'

BISHOPS

A bishop visited one of the churches in his diocese and was dismayed to find that the congregation numbered just nine people. After the service, he spoke to the vicar and complained about the small attendance.

'I'm very disappointed at such a poor turn-out this evening,' said the bishop. 'Did you tell them that I was coming?'

'No,' said the vicar, 'but I fear the news must have leaked out.'

A new young priest was keen to bring the church into the twenty-first century and wanted to introduce a number of modern innovations. One that proved particularly popular was his drive-through confessional.

When the bishop visited, he was greatly impressed by the new service.

'The drive-through confessional is a great idea,' he said. 'It is so convenient for our church members. However, I am afraid we will have to do away with the bright neon sign that says "TOOT and TELL or GO to HELL".'

The archbishop was invited to the bishop's home for dinner one evening and was curious about the bishop's relationship with his house guest, a young actress named Erica. The bishop maintained that he and the actress were just good friends but the archbishop remained suspicious.

A week or so later, the bishop noticed that his cherished silver gravy ladle was missing and he realized that he hadn't seen it since the archbishop came for dinner. After much deliberation, he felt compelled to write to the archbishop: 'I'm not saying you did take the gravy ladle from my house, and I'm not saying you did not take the gravy ladle, but the fact remains that it has been missing ever since you came for dinner.'

A few days later, the bishop received a letter back

from the archbishop. It read: 'I'm not saying that you do sleep with your actress friend, and I'm not saying that you do not sleep with your actress friend, but the fact remains that if she was sleeping in her own bed, she would have found the gravy ladle by now.'

As the Actress said to the Bishop:

(giving golf lessons) 'See how I grip your niblick?'

(getting into a car) 'Do you want to go in the front or the back?'

(doing DIY) 'Have you got something longer?'

(savouring a personal triumph) 'I didn't know I had it in me.'

(inspecting vegetables) 'My God, that's a big one!'

(planting flowers) 'Don't put it in too deep.'

(to a visiting doctor) 'Thank you for coming so quickly.'

(apologizing for a remark) 'It just slipped out.'

(getting caught in a shower of rain) 'I haven't been this wet in ages.'

(inviting in a visitor) 'Why don't you come inside?'

(assembling furniture) 'Insert carefully then slide in all the way.'

As the Bishop said to the Actress:

(giving golf lessons) 'Remember to keep your legs apart.'

(at the dentist) 'You've got the nicest teeth I've ever come across.'

(doing aerobics exercises) 'Squeeze hard on the down stroke.'

(hanging a picture) 'Can you help me to put it up?'

(trying on a suit) 'It's a really tight fit.'

(playing golf) 'It's not often you see a hole like this.'

(to an employee) 'Have you ever handled anything this hard?'

(to an employee) 'I see you've been admiring my equipment.'

(to an employee) 'Is it a bit too stiff for you?'

(offering a sweet) 'Would you like to suck on one of these?'

(peeling an onion) 'It will probably make your eyes water.'

GOD

God was planning a vacation but couldn't decide where to go. 'Why don't you visit Mercury?' suggested an angel.

'Too hot,' said God.

'Well, how about Mars?' ventured the angel.

'Too dry and dusty,' said God.

'You could always try Earth,' said the angel.

'You must be joking!' said God. 'I went there two thousand years ago, knocked up some chick and they're still going on about it.'

At a church harvest festival, the vicar put a sign in front of a pile of freshly baked cakes. It read: 'Please take one cake only – God is watching.'

At the other end of the table sat a display of newly picked apples. A small boy put a sign in front of it, reading: 'Take all the apples you want – God's watching the cakes.'

A devoutly religious man lived next door to an atheist. The religious man prayed three times every day and was always on his knees in communion with the Lord whereas the atheist never went to church. But while the atheist had a well-paid job with a loving wife and family, the pious man lived in poverty with a cheating wife and unruly children.

Feeling a definite sense of injustice, the God-fearing man looked up to heaven and said: 'Lord, I honour you every day without fail and confess my every sin to you, yet you have chosen to make my life miserable. Yet my neighbour, who does not believe, has been rewarded with a prosperous existence. Why is this so, Lord? Why am I not blessed?'

God replied: 'Because you're a bloody pest!'

A little girl walked to and from school every day. Though the weather one morning was ominous and dark clouds were forming, she made the daily trek to the elementary school. As the day progressed, the winds whipped up, along with thunder and lightning. The mother was worried that her daughter would be frightened walking back home from school, and she herself feared the electrical storm might prove dangerous.

Following each roar of the thunder, lightning would cut through the sky like a flaming sword. Being very concerned, the mother got into her car and drove along the route to the school. Soon she saw her small child walking along. The thunder would boom and then, at each flash of lightning, the child would stop, look and smile. One followed another, each time with her child stopping, looking up at the streak of light and smiling.

Finally, the mother called out and asked: 'Honey, what are you doing?'

Her little girl answered: 'God keeps taking pictures of me!'

As a young man, Henry was an exceptional golfer. At the age of twenty-seven, however, he decided to become a priest but joined a very peculiar order.

He took the usual vows of poverty and chastity but his order also required that he quit golf and never play again. This was particularly difficult for Henry but he agreed and was finally ordained as a priest.

One Sunday morning the Reverend Father Henry woke up and, realizing it was an exceptionally beautiful spring day, decided he would play golf.

So he told the associate pastor that he was feeling unwell and convinced him to take Mass for him that day. Then he headed out of town to a golf course fifty miles away where he knew that he was unlikely to meet anyone he knew from his parish.

As Father Henry stood on the first tee, St Peter leaned over to the Lord while looking down from the heavens and exclaimed: 'You're not going to let him get away with this, are you?'

The Lord sighed, and said: 'No, I guess not.'

Just then, Father Henry hit the ball and it shot straight towards the pin, dropping just short of it, rolled up and fell in the hole. It was a 420-yard HOLE-IN-ONE!

St Peter was astonished. He looked at the Lord and asked: 'Why did you let him do that?'

The Lord smiled and replied: 'Who is he going to tell?'

NUNS

Four nuns were gathered in the convent living room and all wanted to watch different programmes on the shared television. The first nun wanted to watch the horse racing, the second nun wanted to watch an exercise show, the third wanted to watch her favourite soap opera and the fourth nun wanted to watch The Nativity. To keep things fair, they decided to watch two minutes of each programme. A fifth nun was walking past the room and heard the following:

'And they're off ...'

'Up and down, up and down ...'

'She's pregnant ...'

'And the baby was born ...'

There were three women who wanted to be nuns. At the end of their training they were told by the head nun to do something really bad then come back and drink from the holy water.

So the trainee nuns went away and came back the next day. The head nun turned to the first trainee and asked: 'What did you do that was bad?'

The first trainee nun replied: 'I booked into a cheap motel room with a married man.' Then she went and drank the holy water.

The head nun asked the second trainee: 'What did you do that was bad?'

The second trainee nun replied: 'I robbed a bank and stole hundreds of pounds.' Then she went and drank from the holy water.

The head nun then asked the third trainee: 'And what did you do that was bad?'

The third trainee nun replied: 'I put cyanide in the holy water.'

THE POPE

A drunk flopped down on a subway seat next to a priest. The drunk's tie was stained, his face was smeared with red lipstick, and a half-empty bottle of Scotch was sticking out of his pocket. He opened his newspaper and began reading. After a few minutes he turned to the priest and said: 'Say, Father, what causes arthritis?'

The priest replied: 'It's caused by loose living, associating with cheap, wicked women, drinking too much alcohol and having contempt for your fellow man.'

'Well, I'll be damned,' the drunk muttered, returning to his paper.

The priest, thinking about what he said, nudged

the man and apologized. 'I'm very sorry, I didn't mean to come on so strong. How long have you had arthritis?'

'I don't have it, Father. I was just reading the Pope does.'

The Pope and the Queen of England were sharing a Dublin stage in their roles as heads of the Catholic and Anglican churches respectively. It was a huge celebration, attended by thousands of people from both sides of the Irish Sea, and there was a gentle rivalry between His Holiness and Her Majesty.

After a few minutes on the stage, the Queen turned to the Pope and said: 'Do you know that with just one little wave of my hand I can make every English person in the crowd go crazy with joy?'

When the Pope expressed doubt, she showed him, and sure enough a wave of her gloved hand brought delirious cheering from every English person in the crowd.

Not wanting to be outdone, the Pope turned to the Queen and said: 'Your Majesty, that was indeed impressive. But do you know that with just one little wave of my hand I can make every Irish person in the crowd go crazy with joy? Furthermore, the joy will not be a momentary display of emotion like that of your subjects but will go deep into their hearts and they will speak forever of this day and recount it to their grandchildren in years to come.'

'One little wave of your hand and the Irish people will rejoice forever?' sniffed the Queen in disbelief. 'Show me.'

So the Pope slapped her in the face.

The Pope had just arrived in New York on a special papal visit. While his luggage was being loaded into the limousine, he waited hesitantly on the pavement.

'Excuse me, Your Holiness,' said his driver. 'Would you please take your seat so that we can leave?'

The Pope looked wistfully at the limo. 'They never let me drive at the Vatican and to tell you the truth, I'd really like to drive today.'

'I'm afraid I can't let you do that,' said the chauffeur. 'I'll lose my job! And what if you had an accident?'

But the Pope was insistent. 'I'll make sure you are handsomely rewarded if you let me drive. Please. Just for this one day.'

Reluctantly, the chauffeur climbed into the back while the Pope positioned himself behind the wheel. No sooner had they left the airport when the Pope put his foot down and soon had the Popemobile doing a-hundred-and-ten miles an hour.

'Slow down, please, Your Holiness!' begged the chauffeur but the Pope kept the pedal to the metal until he heard the sound of police sirens.

'Oh, great!' wailed the suffering chauffeur. 'Now I really will lose my licence!'

As the patrolman approached, the Pope pulled over and rolled down the window. Taking one look at him, the patrolman beat a hasty retreat back to his motorcycle and got straight on the radio.

'I need to talk to the chief,' he said urgently.

The chief of police got on the radio and the patrolman told him that he had stopped a limo that was doing over a-hundred-and-ten miles an hour.

'So bust him,' said the chief.

'I don't think we want to do that,' said the cop. 'He's really important.'

'All the more reason,' replied the chief.

'No, I mean really important,' repeated the cop.

'Who've you got there, the mayor?'

'Bigger.'

'The governor?'

'Bigger.'

'Well,' said the chief, 'who is it?'

'I think it must be God,' replied the flustered cop.

'What on earth makes you think it's God?'

'Well, He's got the Pope driving for Him!'

PRIESTS

A man lived alone in the countryside with only a dog for company. One day the dog died, and the man went to his parish priest and said: 'Father, my dear dog is dead. Could you possibly say a Mass for the poor creature?'

The priest replied: 'I'm afraid not. We cannot have a church service for an animal. But there is a new denomination down the lane and there's no telling what they believe. Maybe they'll do something for your dog.'

'Thank you, Father,' said the man. 'I'll go right away. Do you think five thousand pounds is enough to donate for the service?'

The priest exclaimed: 'Sweet Mary, Mother of Jesus! Why didn't you tell me the dog was Catholic?'

Four Catholic women were enjoying a coffee morning. The first told her friends: 'My son is a priest. When he walks into a room, everyone calls him "Father".'

The second said proudly: 'My son is a bishop. Whenever he walks into a room, people say "Your Grace".'

The third said smugly: 'Well, my son is a cardinal.

Whenever he walks into a room, everyone says "Your Eminence".'

The fourth woman sipped her coffee in silence until the other three turned to her.

'Well …?' They chorused.

Putting her cup down, she said: 'My son is a gorgeous six-foot-tall male stripper. Whenever he walks into a room, everyone says "Oh my God!"'

When a priest was pulled over for speeding, the police officer noticed an empty wine bottle in the car and could smell alcohol on the priest's breath.

'Father, have you been drinking?' asked the officer.

'Only water, my son,' replied the priest.

'Then why can I smell wine?'

The priest looked at the wine bottle and exclaimed: 'Oh my Lord! He's gone and done it again!'

A man joined an order of the priesthood which stipulated that he could not speak for six years, and even then he was only permitted to say two words.

After the first six years of silence, he was led to a small room. His first two words were 'too cold'.

Following another six years of silence, he was taken into the same room and his two words were 'poor food'.

The next six years passed and he was taken back into the room. This time his two words were 'I quit'.

'Good,' said his fellow priest. 'All you have done since you've been here is complain!'

A man went to confession and told the priest that he had been having affairs with women from five neighbouring villages.

'How could you do that?' asked the priest.

'It's easy,' said the man. 'I've got a bicycle!'

A priest was celebrating the twenty-fifth anniversary of his arrival in the parish. To mark the occasion, the church laid on a special evening at the town hall, to be attended by various local dignitaries. Invited to make a little speech of his own, the priest admitted: 'When I first came here, all those years ago, my immediate thoughts were what an awful town this was. For example, although obviously I cannot reveal his identity, the very first person who entered my confessional told me how he had stolen money from the school charity box, vandalized the park greenhouse and had been having an affair with the wife of the factory owner. But, thankfully, I soon discovered that he was an isolated case and that this town has many warm-hearted souls.'

As others then paid tribute to the priest's unstinting service to the community, the mayor, who was making the main speech, apologized for arriving late. Taking to the stage, he began: 'I well remember Father O'Grady's arrival in this town twenty-five years ago. As a matter of fact, I had the honour of being the first person to go to him in confession ...'.

A priest was walking along the corridor of the parochial school near the pre-school wing when a group of small boys were passing on the way to the cafeteria. One little lad of about three stopped and looked at him in his clerical clothes and asked: 'Why do you dress funny?'

He told him that he was a priest and that this is the uniform priests wear.

Then the boy pointed to the priest's collar tab and asked: 'Have you cut yourself?'

The priest was perplexed until he realized that to the little boy the collar tab looked like a plaster. So the priest took it out and handed it to the boy to show him. On the back of the tab were letters giving the name of the manufacturer.

The young boy felt the letters, and the priest asked: 'Do you know what those words say?'

'Yes, I do,' said the boy, who was not yet old enough to read. Peering intently at the letters he said: 'Kills ticks and fleas for up to six months.'

A new priest was nervous about hearing confessions, so he asked an older priest to sit in on his sessions. After the young man had heard several confessions, the older priest asked him to step out of the confessional so that he could give him a few suggestions.

The older priest advised: 'Cross your arms over your chest and rub your chin with one hand.'

So the new priest tried out the gesture.

'That's good,' said the old priest. 'Now try saying things like, "I see, yes, go on" and "I understand, how did you feel about that?"'

The new priest repeated what his colleague said and nodded sagely.

The old priest concluded: 'Now don't you think that's a little better than slapping your knee and saying: "You're kidding! What happened next?"'

RABBIS

A priest and a rabbi worked at a church and a synagogue on opposite sides of the street from each other. As they often had to visit the same parts of town, they decided to club together and buy a car.

Returning from the car showroom, they parked their new car on the street roughly midway between the church and the synagogue. A few minutes later, the rabbi looked out of the synagogue and saw the priest sprinkling water on the car.

'What are you doing?' he asked. 'It's brand new. It doesn't need washing yet.'

'I'm blessing it,' replied the priest.

After considering the spiritual significance of the priest's actions, the rabbi went back inside the synagogue and reappeared a minute later with a hacksaw. He then walked over to the back of the car and cut two inches off the exhaust pipe.

A smiling rabbi said to one of his friends: 'I gladdened seven hearts today.'

'Seven hearts?' said the friend. 'How did you manage that?'

'I performed three marriages,' replied the rabbi.

The friend looked at him quizzically. 'Seven

hearts? Six I could understand but ...'

'What do you think?' interjected the rabbi. 'That I do this for free?'

A priest, a Methodist preacher and a rabbi were talking about how they divided up the collection money.

The priest said: 'I draw a line down the centre of the room, then I throw the collection money up in the air. Whatever lands on the left side of the line belongs to God and whatever lands on the right side is mine.'

The preacher said: 'I draw a circle in the centre of the room, then I throw the collection money up in the air. Whatever lands in the circle is God's and the rest is mine.'

The rabbi smiled and said: 'I throw the collection money as high in the air as I can and tell God to take what he wants. Whatever comes back down is mine.'

School

It was at the end of the school year and a kindergarten teacher was receiving gifts from her pupils.

The florist's son handed her a wrapped gift. She shook it, held it overhead and said: 'I bet I know what it is. Some flowers.'

'That's right,' the boy said, 'but how did you know?'

'Oh, just a wild guess,' she smiled.

The next pupil was the sweet shop owner's daughter. The teacher held up her wrapped gift, shook it and said: 'I bet I can guess what it is. A box of sweets.'

'That's right, but how did you know?' asked the girl.

'Oh, just a wild guess,' smiled the teacher.

The next gift was from the son of the liquor store owner. The teacher held the wrapped package overhead but it was leaking. She touched a drop of the leakage with her finger and held it to her tongue.

'Is it wine?' she asked.

'No,' the boy replied, with some excitement.

The teacher repeated the process, taking a larger drop of the leakage to her tongue.

'Is it champagne?' she asked.

'No,' the boy replied, even more excitedly.

The teacher took one more taste before declaring: 'I give up, what is it?'

With great glee, the boy replied: 'It's a puppy!'

The teacher came up with a good problem. 'Suppose,' she asked the class, 'there were a dozen sheep and six of them jumped over a fence. How many would be left?'

'None,' answered little Sammy.

'None? Sammy, you don't know your arithmetic.'

Johnny replied: 'Miss, you don't know your sheep. When one goes, they all go!'

Teacher: Johnny, why are you doing your work on the floor?

Johnny: Because you said to do this maths problem without tables.

'Isn't the head a dummy?' said a boy to a girl.

'Well, do you know who I am?' asked the girl.

'No,' replied the boy.

'I'm the head's daughter,' said the girl.

'And do you know who I am?' asked the boy.

'No,' she replied.

'Thank goodness!' said the boy with a sigh of relief.

Teacher: If I give you two rabbits and two rabbits and another two rabbits, how many rabbits have you got?

Patty: Seven!

Teacher: No, listen carefully again. If I give you two rabbits and two rabbits and another two rabbits, how many rabbits have you got?

Patty: Seven!

Teacher: Let's try this another way. If I give you two apples and two apples and another two apples, how many apples have you got?

Patty: Six.

Teacher: Good. Now if I give you two rabbits and two rabbits and another two rabbits, how many rabbits have you got?

Patty: Seven!

Teacher: How on earth do you work out that three lots of two rabbits is seven?

Patty: I've already got one rabbit at home!

Little Jimmy's kindergarten class was on a field trip to their local police station where they saw pictures tacked to a bulletin board of the ten most wanted men. One of the youngsters pointed to a picture and asked if it really was the photo of a wanted person.

'Yes,' said the police officer. 'The detectives want him very badly.'

Hearing this, Jimmy asked: 'So why didn't you keep him when you took his picture?'

One day, during a lesson on grammar, the teacher asked for a show of hands from those who could use the word 'beautiful' in the same sentence twice.

First, she called on little Suzie, who responded

with: 'My father bought my mother a beautiful dress and she looked beautiful in it.'

'Very good, Suzie,' said the teacher. She then called on little Michael who said: 'My mummy planned a beautiful banquet and it turned out beautifully.'

'Excellent, Michael!' said the teacher.

Then the teacher called on little Freddy who thought for a moment and said: 'Last night, at the dinner table, my sister told my father that she was pregnant and he said, "Beautiful ... just bloody beautiful!"'

The kindergarten class were given a homework assignment to find out about something exciting and relate it to the class the next day. When the time came for the children to give their reports, the teacher called on them one at a time. She was reluctant to call upon little Bobby, knowing that he sometimes could be a bit crude. But eventually his turn came.

Little Bobby walked up to the front of the class and, with a piece of chalk, made a small white dot on the blackboard, then sat back down. The teacher couldn't figure out what Bobby had in mind for his report, so she asked him about the significance of the dot.

'It's a period,' reported Bobby.

'Well, I can see that,' she said. 'But what is so exciting about a period?'

'Damned if I know,' said Bobby, 'but this morning my sister said she missed one. Then Daddy had a heart attack, Mummy fainted and the man next door shot himself!'

It was the end of the school year. The teacher had turned in her grades and was nothing really for the class to do. All the kids were restless and it was near the end of the day. So the teacher thought of an activity.

She said: 'The first ones to answer correctly the questions I ask may leave early today.'

Little Joe said to himself: 'Good, I'm smart and I want to get out of here.'

The teacher asked: 'Who said, "Four score and seven years ago"?'

Before Joe could open his mouth, Susie said: 'Abraham Lincoln.'

'That's right, Susie,' said the teacher. 'You may go.'

Joe was really mad that Susie had answered first.

Then the teacher asked: 'Who said, "I have a dream"?'

But before Joe could open his mouth, Mary said: 'Martin Luther King.'

'That's right, Mary,' said the teacher. 'You may go.'

Joe was even madder than before because Mary had answered first.

Then the teacher asked: 'Who said, "Ask not what your country can do for you"?'

Before Joe could open his mouth, Nancy piped up: 'John Kennedy.'

The teacher said: 'That's right, Nancy. You may go.'

Now Joe was furious!

The teacher turned her back and Joe muttered: 'I wish these bitches would keep their mouths shut!'

The teacher spun around. 'Who said that?' she demanded.

Joe replied: 'Bill Clinton. Can I go now?'

One day, the teacher decided that in science class she would give a lesson about the elements. So she stood in the front of the class and said: 'Children, if you could have one raw element in the world what would it be?'

Stevie raised his hand and said: 'I would want gold, because gold is worth a lot of money and I could buy a Porsche.'

The teacher nodded and then called on Susie who said: 'I would want platinum because platinum is worth more than gold and I could buy a Ferrari.'

The teacher smiled and then called on Johnny who stood up and said: 'I would want silicon.'

The teacher asked: 'Why, Johnny?'

He said: 'Because my mum has two bags of it and you should see all the sports cars outside our house!'

Little Johnny was being questioned by the teacher during an arithmetic lesson. 'If you had ten pounds,' said the teacher, 'and I asked you for a loan of eight pounds, how much would you have left?'

'Ten pounds,' said Johnny firmly.

'Ten?' the teacher asked. 'How do you make it ten?'

'Well,' replied Johnny, 'you may ask for a loan of eight pounds but that doesn't mean you'll get it!'

Sex

After his wife disappeared suddenly from their home without explanation, a worried husband contacted all her friends and scoured the entire neighbourhood in his search for her. When this proved fruitless, he reported her to the police as a missing person. Then three days later, he returned home to find her standing in the bathroom.

'Darling,' he cried, throwing his arms around her in relief. 'Where have you been? I've been worried out of my mind.'

She said: 'Six men in black ski masks broke into the house, kidnapped me, bundled me into a car, bound and gagged me and kept me in a room where they had rough sex with me for a week.'

'But you've only been gone three days,' said the husband, puzzled. 'What do you mean, a week?'

She replied: 'I'm only here to collect my toothbrush.'

A man was about to have sex with a really fat woman. After climbing on top of her, he asked: 'Can I turn the light off?'

'Is it because you're a bit shy?' she said.

'No,' he said. 'It's because it's burning my ass!'

A seventeen-year-old boy was riding the bus home from college and there was a gorgeous blonde girl sat across the aisle from him. He kept checking her out but lacked the nerve to talk to her. Suddenly she sneezed and her glass eye came flying out of its socket towards him. He reached out and snatched it out of the air.

'Oh my God, I am so sorry,' the girl said as she popped her eye back into place. 'Let me buy you dinner to make it up to you.'

They enjoyed a wonderful dinner together and afterwards the girl invited him to go with her to a movie. She paid for everything, including a taxi cab ride for the two of them to her house.

She kissed him passionately and asked him if he wanted to stay the night. He readily agreed and they enjoyed fantastic sex.

The next morning, he felt compelled to ask her: 'Do you make a habit of sleeping with guys you've only just met?'

'No,' she replied. 'You just happened to catch my eye.'

A man in a bar began chatting up an attractive woman. Eventually he said: 'Can I ask you a personal question? How many men have you slept with?'

'I'm not telling you that,' she replied. 'That's my business.'

'Sorry,' he said. 'I didn't realize you made a living out of it.'

The census-taker rang a doorbell and was surprised to be greeted by a naked woman. 'Don't be alarmed,' she said. 'I'm a nudist.'

Although embarrassed by the situation, the man proceeded to ask the standard questions. 'How many children do you have?' he asked.

'Seventeen,' replied the woman.

'Lady,' he gasped, 'you're not a nudist, you just don't have time to get dressed!'

'I don't know what to get my wife for her birthday,' said a man to his friend. 'She has everything and, besides, she can afford to buy anything she wants.'

His friend said: 'I have an idea. Why don't you make up a certificate that entitles her to two hours of great sex, any way she wants it. She'll love that.'

'That's a great idea,' said the man, and he went about drawing up the certificate.

The next day his friend asked: 'Well, how did it go? Did your wife like the certificate?'

'Oh, yes, she loved it,' said the man. 'She jumped up, thanked me, kissed me on the mouth and ran out of the house yelling: "I'll see you in two hours".'

After a woman had swallowed a Super Gillette razor blade, her doctor discovered that not only had she given herself a tonsillectomy, an appendectomy and a hysterectomy, but she had also castrated her husband, circumcized her lover, taken two fingers off a casual acquaintance, given the vicar a hair lip – and there were still five shaves left!

A woman sat down on a park bench and, seeing nobody around, decided to stretch out her legs on the seat and relax. A few minutes later, a tramp came up to her and said: 'Hey, gorgeous, how about you and me get it together?'

'How dare you!' she said. 'I'm not one of your cheap pick-ups!'

'In that case,' said the tramp, 'what are you doing in my bed?'

Worried about his performance in bed, a middle-aged man consulted his doctor who prescribed him Viagra and told him to take it half an hour before sex. The man collected his prescription and went home to wait for his wife to return from her shopping trip. Half an hour before she was due home, he took the Viagra pill but shortly afterwards she phoned to say that she had been delayed a couple of hours.

Seized with panic, he called the doctor. 'What should I do? I've taken the pill but the effects will have worn off by the time my wife gets home.'

'Well,' said the doctor, 'it's a shame to waste it. Do you have a maid?'

'Yes.'

'Could you not amuse yourself with her instead?'

'I guess so,' said the man. 'But I don't need Viagra with the maid.'

A market researcher knocked on the door of a house and was greeted by a young woman with three small children running around at her feet.

'Excuse me, Madam,' he said, 'I'm doing some research for Vaseline. Have you ever used the product?'

'Yes,' she replied. 'My husband and I use it all the time.'

'If you don't mind me asking, what do you use it for?'

'We use it for sex,' said the woman.

The researcher was taken aback by her candour. He said: 'Usually people lie to me and say they use it on a child's bicycle chain or to ease a gate hinge, whereas I know for a fact that most people do use it for sex. I admire you for your honesty and since you have been so frank with me, can you tell me exactly how you use it for sex?'

'Certainly,' said the wife. 'My husband and I put it on our bedroom door knob to keep the kids out.'

A man was riding through the desert on a camel. After a while the heat and loneliness got to him and he developed an overwhelming urge to have sex. Since there were no women in the desert, he turned to his camel. He tried to position himself to have sex with the camel but the animal ran off. When he caught the camel, he climbed back on and rode on through the desert.

Soon, however, the urge for sex returned, stronger than ever. Once more he turned to his camel and tried to get in a position to have sex with it but again the animal ran off. He managed to catch it, climbed back on and rode on through the desert.

Finally he came to a road and saw a broken down car with three beautiful voluptuous blondes sitting in it. One of the girls came over to him and said: 'If you fix our car, we'll do anything you want.'

Luckily the man knew a lot about cars and was soon able to get it going. As the engine started up, the three girls smiled: 'How can we ever repay you, mister?'

The man thought for a moment and said: 'Will you hold my camel?'

Two old ladies at a dance. One said: 'Do you remember the minuet?'

The other said: 'I can't even remember the ones I screwed.'

How they have sex:

Accountants are good with figures.
Actors do it on cue.
Ambulance drivers come quicker.
Assembly line workers do it over and over.
Bakers knead it daily.
Bankers impose a penalty for early withdrawal.
Bartenders call the shots.
Bookkeepers enjoy double entry.
Bridge players try to get a rubber.
Bus drivers come early and pull out on time.
Chess players check their mates.
Doctors do it with patience.
Drummers do it in 4/4 time.
Dustmen come once a week.
Farmers spread it around.
Firemen are always in heat.
Gas station attendants pump all day.
Insurance salesmen are premium lovers.
Jockeys like to come first.
Landscapers plant it deeper.
Lawyers charge by the hour.
Milkmen deliver twice a week.
Photocopiers reproduce the fastest.
Pilots keep it up longer.
Policemen like big busts.
Postmen come slower.

Printers do it without wrinkling the sheets.
Reporters do it daily.
Roofers do it on top.
Sailors like to be blown.
Skydivers are good till the last drop.
Tailors make it fit.
Taxidermists mount anything.
Writers have novel ways.

A young man went into a pharmacy to buy some condoms. The pharmacist explained that the condoms were in packs of three, nine or twelve and asked the young man which he wanted.

'Well,' said the young man, 'I've been seeing this girl for a while and she's really hot. We're having dinner with her parents tonight and then we're going out, and I've a feeling I'm going to get lucky. And once we start there'll be no stopping us. So I'll take the pack of twelve.'

He bought the condoms and left.

That evening he sat down to dinner with his girlfriend and her parents. Before they ate, he asked whether he might be allowed to say grace and then proceeded to launch into a long prayer. At the end of it his girlfriend leaned over and whispered to him: 'I didn't know you were religious.'

The young man whispered back: 'And I didn't know your father was a pharmacist.'

'Hey, you look different today, Kelly!' said one of her co-workers. 'Your hair is extra curly and you have this wide-eyed look. What did you use – special curlers and some dramatic eye make-up?'

'No,' replied Kelly. 'My vibrator shorted out this morning.'

A young man went on a blind date with a girl at an amusement park. After they went for a ride on the big wheel, she seemed bored, so he asked her: 'What would you like to do next?'

'I wanna be weighed,' she said.

So he took her over to the weighing machine.

Then they rode the roller coaster and he bought her some popcorn. 'What do you fancy doing now?' he asked.

'I wanna be weighed,' she said.

Realizing that someone so obsessed with her weight wasn't right for him, he feigned a headache and took her home early.

The girl's mother was surprised to see her back so soon.

'What's wrong, dear?' she asked. 'How was your date?'

'Wousy,' said the girl.

SHOW BUSINESS

A man went to his local video store and said: 'Can I take The Elephant Man out?'

The sales clerk said: 'He's not your type.'

Sean Connery's career had hit the rocks but then, one day out of the blue, his agent rang and said: 'Sean, I've got a job for you. It starts tomorrow but you've got to be there early, about tennish.'

Connery frowned: 'Tennish? But I haven't even got a racket!'

Just a day after two actors had got married, the groom filed for divorce.

His lawyer was puzzled. 'How can your marriage be on the rocks already? You've barely been married a day.'

'I could tell at the church that it would be an impossible relationship,' said the actor grandly, 'when she signed her name in the register in bigger letters than mine.'

A man walked into a grocery store and said: 'I want to buy every rotten egg you've got.'

'Why would you want to buy rotten eggs?' asked the shopkeeper. 'No one wants rotten eggs, unless you're going to see that lousy comedian at the club across the street.'

'I know,' said the man. 'I am the lousy comedian at the club across the street.'

A man lay spread out over three seats in the fifth row of a movie theatre. Spotting this, an usher marched over and said: 'What do you think you're doing, taking up three seats? Have you no manners? Where did you come from?'

The man looked up helplessly and said: 'The balcony!'

A man went into a video store and asked: 'Can I borrow Batman Forever?'

The sales clerk said: 'No, you'll have to bring it back tomorrow.'

What's the difference between an actor and a pizza?
—A pizza can feed a family of four.

How can you tell when a plane is full of actors?
—When the engine stops but the whining continues.

A small boy was performing in a school play when he suddenly fell through a trap-door.

The audience gasped but the boy's mother calmly turned to her friend and said: 'Don't worry. It's just a stage he's going through.'

A drunk walked up to a barman and said: 'If I show you a trick will you give me a free Scotch?'

The barman replied: 'It depends how good a trick it is.'

The drunk reached into his pocket, pulled out a frog and placed it behind the piano. The frog started to play the sweetest jazz riff the barman had ever heard. So he poured the drunk his Scotch.

After downing his Scotch, the drunk said: 'If I show you another trick can I have another free one?'

The bartender said: 'If it's anything like that last one, you can drink free all night.'

The drunk reached into his other pocket, pulled out a rat, set it on top of the piano, and the rat started singing in tune with the frog.

Impressed, the barman started to pour drinks as fast as the drunk could knock them back. After several hours, a big time Hollywood agent walked in, saw the act and frantically asked the barman who it belonged to. The barman pointed to the drunk who was passed out on the floor.

The agent woke him up and said: 'I will give you one million pounds for that act.'

The drunk slurred: 'Not for sale.'

The agent said: 'Okay, how about two hundred thousand pounds for the singing rat?'

The drunk replied: 'It's a deal.'

The agent wrote out the cheque and left with the rat.

The barman looked at the drunk and said: 'Are you nuts? You had a million pound act that you broke up for just two hundred grand!'

The drunk replied: 'Relax, the frog is a ventriloquist!'

After another tough day looking for work, a struggling actor returned home to find that his house had burned to the ground. As emergency crews doused the last of the flames, the actor went over to the fire chief to ask what had happened.

'Well,' said the fire chief, 'it seems that your agent came by your house earlier today and while he was here he molested your wife, hit your children, kicked your dog and burned your house to the ground.'

The actor was rendered speechless, his jaw hanging open in disbelief. 'My agent came to my house …?'

Sport

BASEBALL

A baseball fan bought a ticket for the big game but when he arrived in the stadium he found that his seat had a restricted view behind a pillar. Spotting an empty seat with a much better view in the next row, he made his way there and asked the man sitting in the adjacent seat whether the empty seat was taken.

'This is my wife's seat,' he said sadly. 'She passed away. She was a big fan.'

'I'm sorry to hear about your loss. May I ask why you didn't give the ticket to a friend or a relative?'

'They're all at the funeral.'

How do baseball players stay cool?
—They sit next to their fans.

By the time Ted arrived for the baseball game he had missed more than half an hour.

'Why are you so late?' asked his friend.

'I had to toss a coin to decide whether I went to church or came to the game.'

'How come you took so long?'

'Well,' said Ted, 'I had to toss it seventeen times.'

BOXING

A boxer with an insomnia problem went to see a doctor.

'Have you tried counting sheep?' suggested the doctor.

'It doesn't work,' said the boxer. 'Whenever I get to nine, I stand up!'

GOLF

A bride was waiting anxiously outside church when the groom finally showed up, carrying a set of golf clubs.

'Why have you brought your golf clubs to our wedding?' she yelled.

'Well,' he said, 'this isn't going to take all afternoon, is it?'

A professional golfer who was having a bad round eventually took out his frustration on his caddie. 'Would you mind not checking your watch after every shot – it's distracting.'

'It's not a watch,' replied the caddie frostily. 'It's a compass.'

Why do golfers wear two pairs of socks?
—In case they get a hole in one.

After his cruise ship sank, a retired business executive ended up stranded on a desert island for eight years. During that time he didn't see another living person until one day, out of the blue, a beautiful woman rowed her boat onto his beach.

'Where did you come from?' he asked incredulously. 'How did you get here?'

'I rowed from the other side of the island,' she said. 'I got washed up here when my cruise ship sank.'

'That's amazing,' he said. 'To think, you've been here all this time! You were lucky that a boat washed up with you.'

'Oh, no,' she said. 'I made that myself from raw materials I found on the island. I've also built my own house. Would you like to see it?'

The man could hardly believe what was happening as he climbed into her boat and she rowed them to the far side of the island. Stepping ashore there, he saw a magnificent bungalow before him. He was stunned.

'Come inside,' she smiled. 'Would you like a drink?'

'I'm not sure I could face another coconut juice today,' he said.

'Don't worry, I made my own still. How about a pina colada?'

She poured his drink and came to sit next to him on the couch. 'I bet you've been really lonely these past eight years,' she purred, stroking his leg. 'I'm sure there's something you'd love to do right now – something you've been longing for?'

He gasped excitedly: 'Don't tell me you've built a golf course!'

355

A little old lady owned a home beside the fifth fairway of a local golf course and stray golf balls were always landing in her back yard. Instead of getting angry, she removed the fence along the boundary, invited the golfers onto her property, showed them where their ball was located and encouraged them to take their next shot from that spot. Even when they missed and dug deep holes in her lawn, she would tell them to go ahead and take another swing.

A visitor, after witnessing her overly courteous behaviour, couldn't help but comment. 'How come you let them tear up your yard like that?' he asked. 'And not only that, you encourage them!'

'I'm not as courteous as you think,' the old lady replied. 'I'm planning on turning my yard into a vegetable garden, and I figure that within another month they'll have it ploughed for me!'

Two golfers were talking in the clubhouse. 'You won't believe this,' said one, 'but I got a set of golf clubs for my wife.'

'Great swap!' said the other.

Two friends were playing golf. One said: 'Hey, that's a smart new ball you've got there.'

'It's the latest gadget,' said the other. 'It's a golf ball that's impossible to lose. If it goes in bushes or trees, it lights up; if it lands in water, it sends a constant ripple to the surface; and if you're playing at night, it emits a bleeping sound to help you find it. It's going to revolutionize the game.'

'That's fantastic. Where did you get it?'

'I found it.'

A married couple were playing golf together at their local course as they did most days. The husband was standing on the first tee and his wife was standing some fifteen yards ahead on the ladies' tee. He teed off first and hit the ball sweetly but unfortunately it smacked into the back of his wife's head, killing her instantly.

At the resultant inquest, the coroner said there was no doubt that cause of death was being hit by a golf ball, and there was even a perfect imprint of a Topflite No. 1 ball on the back of the wife's head.

'Yes,' confirmed the husband. 'That was my ball.'

'However,' continued the coroner, 'I was disturbed to hear that a Maxfli Vt2 golf ball was found inserted up the deceased's backside. Could you throw some light on this?'

'Oh, I wondered where that went,' said the husband. 'That was my provisional.'

SOCCER

A wife was having an affair with a television repairman. She told him: 'My husband totally ignores me. All he wants to do is watch the match on television. That's why we've got such a ridiculously large set.'

Just then, she heard a key in the front door. It was her husband. 'Quick!' she said to her lover. 'Hide in the back of the TV!'

So her lover hid in the television while the husband settled down to watch the match. But after fifteen minutes, it became so hot and uncomfortable in the back of the television set that the lover could bear it no longer. Throwing caution to the wind, he simply climbed out of the set, walked straight past the husband and out the front door.

The husband turned to his wife and said: 'Hey, honey, I didn't see the referee send off that guy, did you?'

In a restaurant kitchen, a swarm of flies were playing soccer in a saucer. After they had finished, one fly turned to another and said: 'You'll have to play better than that tomorrow.'

'Why?'

'Because tomorrow we're playing in the cup.'

Shortly before kick-off, the coach of an under-nines soccer team went over to one of his young players and said: 'You do understand that you mustn't swear at the referee if he gives you a card, and that you mustn't hit one of the other team if he fouls you?'

'Yes, I understand,' said the boy.

'Good,' said the coach. 'Now go and explain it to your mother.'

TRAVEL

A humble farmer and his wife visited a big city air fair. Although he had never flown before, the farmer had long been fascinated by planes and so he decided to ask the pilot of a small aircraft what it would cost for a ride.

'Two hundred pounds,' replied the pilot.

'That's a lot of money,' said the farmer. 'I just don't think I can afford that much, which is a real pity because I've always wanted to go up in one of those things.'

The pilot was impressed by such obvious enthusiasm and suggested a deal. 'How about I let you and your wife ride free on one condition – that you don't make a sound at any time during the flight? If I hear you make a sound, it'll cost you the full two hundred pounds.'

The couple agreed and climbed into the plane. The pilot went through his full repertoire of tricks, performing spectacular twists, loops and dives. Forty minutes later, as he touched down on the runway, he asked the farmer if he had enjoyed it.

'It was amazing,' said the farmer. 'Thank you.'

'Well, I must congratulate you on your bravery,' said the pilot. 'I did all those daredevil aerial stunts and you didn't utter a sound the whole trip.'

'It was a close call though,' admitted the farmer. 'I almost said something when my wife fell out.'

What do you call the drivers in an Egyptian traffic jam?
—Tootin-car-men.

A man with no legs was waiting at a bus stop. The bus driver pulled up and shouted: 'How are you getting on, Bill?'

A husband and wife were on safari in Africa.

'Look!' exclaimed the husband excitedly. 'Lion tracks! You see where they go and I'll find out where they came from.'

A man was driving along the road when he saw a police car behind flashing him to stop. As he stepped out of the car to see what the problem was, he threw up his hands in horror.

The officer said: 'I'm afraid your rear lights aren't working properly.'

'I don't believe it!' shouted the man. 'I just can't believe this has happened!'

'There's no need to get so agitated,' said the officer. 'The lights can be fixed at a garage.'

'Never mind about the lights!' exclaimed the man. 'Where's my caravan?'

A man had been driving all night and by morning was still far from his destination. He decided to stop at the next city he came to and park somewhere quiet so he could get an hour or two of sleep. Unfortunately for him, the quiet place he chose happened to be on one of the city's major jogging routes. No sooner had he settled back to snooze when there came a knocking on his window. He looked out and saw a jogger standing outside.

'Yes?' the man asked, annoyed at being disturbed.

'Excuse me, sir,' the jogger said. 'Do you have the time?'

The man looked at the car clock and answered: 'It's quarter past eight.'

The jogger said thanks and left. The man settled back again and was just dozing off when there was another knock on the window and another jogger.

'Excuse me, sir, do you have the time?'

'It's half past eight,' replied the man grumpily.

The jogger said thanks and left. Now the man could see other joggers passing by and he knew it was only a matter of time before another one disturbed him. To avoid the problem, he got out a pen and paper and put a sign in his window saying: 'I do not know the time.'

Once again he settled back to sleep. He was just dozing off when there was another knock on the window.

'Sir, sir! It's quarter to nine.'

Two men were discussing past holidays. One said: 'I remember about five years ago we stayed at a hotel in Bournemouth.'

'In Dorset?' asked the other.

'Definitely. I'd recommend it to anyone.'

A photographer who specialized in taking aerial shots of the landscape booked an hour-long flight at a small airfield. When he arrived he was told that his plane was waiting for him and so, spotting a plane with its engine running, he climbed in.

'Okay,' he said to the pilot. 'Let's go.'

Once airborne, the photographer said: 'I'd like you to come in low over that forest so I can take some nice pictures.'

'Why do you want to take photos?' asked the pilot.

'It's my job. I'm a photographer.'

'Oh,' said the pilot. 'So you're not the flight instructor?'

Taking his wife for an afternoon drive, a man roared along a narrow country lane at breakneck speed.

'Can't you slow down when you're turning corners?' she cried. 'You're scaring me to death!'

'Just do what I do,' he replied. 'Shut your eyes.'

How do you double the value of a Lada?
—Put a gallon of petrol in it.

What do you call a Lada with twin exhausts?
—A wheelbarrow.

What occupies the last ten pages of the Lada Owners'
Handbook?
—The bus and train timetables.

What's the difference between a Jehovah's Witness
and a Lada?
—You can shut the door on a Lada.

What do you call the shock absorbers on a Lada?
—Passengers.

What do you call a Lada at the top of a hill?
—A miracle.

What's the difference between flu and a Lada?
—You can get rid of flu.

Why do Ladas have two spare wheels?
—So you can cycle home.

A man and a woman were driving along the same road from opposite directions. As they passed, the woman leaned out of her car window and yelled: 'Pig!'

The man angrily responded by leaning out of his window and shouting: 'Bitch!'

Each continued on their way until the man rounded the next corner and crashed into a huge pig standing in the middle of the road.

The passengers on a plane were waiting for the pilot to arrive so that they could take off. Eventually the pilot and co-pilot boarded at the rear of the plane and began walking down the aisle towards the cockpit. However, the passengers were alarmed to see that both men appeared to be blind. The pilot had a white stick and kept bumping into people as he stumbled down the aisle, while his co-pilot used a guide dog.

So the passengers were understandably apprehensive as the plane's engines revved up. As it started to accelerate, many began to pray. Closer and closer it got to the end of the runway. Voices were becoming more hysterical. With less than twenty feet of runway left, everyone on board screamed and at the very last minute the plane rose into the sky.

Up in the cockpit the co-pilot let out a huge sigh of relief. Turning to the pilot, he said: 'You know, one of these days the passengers aren't going to scream, and we won't know when to take off!'

A man said to his friend: 'My wife and I can't agree on our holiday. I want to go to Bermuda but she wants to come with me.'

'The car won't start,' sighed a wife to her husband. 'I think there must be water in the carburettor.'

'How do you know?' sneered the husband. 'You don't even know what the carburettor is!'

'Have it your way!' said the wife. 'But I'm sure there's water in the carburettor.'

'We'll see,' said the husband condescendingly. 'I'll check it out. Where's the car?'

'In the river.'

Sherlock Holmes and Doctor Watson went on a camping trip. After a good meal and a bottle of wine, they lay down for the night and went to sleep. Some hours later, Holmes awoke and nudged his faithful friend.

'Watson, look up at the sky and tell me what you see,' he said.

Watson replied: 'I see millions and millions of stars.'

'What does that tell you?' inquired Holmes.

Watson pondered for a minute before answering: 'Astronomically, it tells me that there are millions of galaxies and potentially billions of planets. Astrologically, I observe that Saturn is in Leo. Horologically, I deduce that the time is approximately a quarter past three. Theologically, I can see that God is all powerful and that we are small and insignificant. Meteorologically, I suspect that we will have a beautiful clear day tomorrow. What does it tell you, Holmes?'

Holmes replied wearily: 'What it tells me, Watson, you idiot, is that someone has stolen our tent!'

One taxi driver said to another: 'Why is one side of your cab painted black and the other red?'

'It makes good sense. When I get in an accident, the police always believe my version of events because the witnesses contradict each other.'

Tom and Ted were debating whether the island where they were staying on holiday was pronounced 'Hawaii' or 'Havaii'.

'It's Hawaii,' said Tom.

'No, it's Havaii,' insisted Ted.

Eventually they decided to resolve the dispute by asking a passer-by, who answered 'Havaii'.

'Thank you,' smiled Ted.

'You're velcome,' replied the passer-by.

A man was being interviewed for a job as a railway signalman. The interviewer asked: 'What would you do if two trains were approaching each other on the same line?'

'I'd switch the points in the signal box,' replied the candidate.

'But what if the signal switch was broken?'

'Then I'd use the manual lever.'

'But what if that was broken, too?'

'I'd use the emergency phone to alert the next signal box up the line,' said the candidate confidently.

'But what if there was no answer?' pressed the interviewer.

'Well, in that case I'd ring my dad and tell him to come over.'

'What good would that do?' asked the interviewer.

'None,' said the candidate. 'But he's never seen a train crash!'

A man arrived home from work to find his wife waiting for him. She sat him down and told him she had good news and bad news about the car.

'Okay,' he said apprehensively. 'What's the good news?'

She said: 'The air bag works.'

An irate motorist returned to the garage where he had bought an expensive battery for his car four months earlier. He told the garage owner: 'When I bought that battery, you said it would be the last one my car would ever need. Now four months later, it's dead.'

'I'm sorry,' said the garage owner. 'I just didn't think your car would last longer than that.'

A passenger on an airplane was sweating like a pig, fidgeting constantly and biting his nails. Aware of his discomfort, the flight attendant said: 'Sir, can I get you something from the trolley bar to ease your nerves?'

She fetched him a whisky and he downed it in one but fifteen minutes later she noticed that his entire body was shaking.

'Would another whisky help?' she asked.

'Yes, please,' he spluttered. So she brought him another whisky and he knocked it back.

But ten minutes later he seemed worse than ever and had started sobbing loudly. The flight attendant said: 'I've never seen anyone so scared of flying.'

'I'm not scared of flying,' said the passenger. 'I'm trying to give up drink!'

A truck driver was speeding along the road when he suddenly spotted a sign that said: 'Low Bridge Ahead.' In desperation he slammed on the brakes but he was going too fast to stop and ended up wedging his vehicle under the bridge.

Ten minutes later, a police car appeared on the scene. The officer went over to the truck driver and said sarcastically: 'So you got stuck, eh?'

'No,' replied the truck driver, 'I was delivering this bridge and ran out of fuel.'

Waiters

A customer walked into an ice cream parlour and asked what flavours they served.

'Chocolate, vanilla and strawberry,' replied the waitress in a hoarse voice.

Attempting to be sympathetic, the customer asked: 'Do you have laryngitis?'

'No,' said the waitress. 'Just chocolate, vanilla and strawberry.'

At the height of the tourist season, an out-of-towner in New York decided to visit an uptown restaurant he had liked on a previous visit to the city. Finally catching the eye of an overworked waiter, he said: 'You know, it's been over five years since I first came in here.'

'Well, you'll have to wait your turn, sir,' replied the harassed waiter. 'I can only serve one table at a time.'

A waiter at a down-at-heel restaurant asked his two customers whether they wanted wine with their meal.

'Yes, I'll have a glass of red,' said the first.

'I'll have red, too,' said the second, 'and make sure the glass is clean.'

Five minutes later the waiter returned with the drinks. 'Two red wines,' he announced. 'Now which one of you asked for the clean glass?'

Customer: I thought the meals here were supposed to be like mother used to make.
Waiter: They are. She couldn't cook either.

Customer: Look out, waiter! Your thumb is in my soup!
Waiter: Don't worry, sir. It's not hot.

Customer: Give me a hot dog.
Waiter: With pleasure.
Customer: No, with mustard.

Customer: This salad is frozen solid!
Waiter: It's the iceberg lettuce that does it.

Customer: I'd like a cup of coffee with no cream.
Waiter: Sorry, sir, we're out of cream. Would you like your coffee with no milk instead?

Customer: Waiter, can you get rid of this fly in my starter?
Waiter: I can't do that. He hasn't had his main course yet.

Customer: Waiter, there's a fly in my sauce!
Waiter: No, sir, that's a cockroach. The fly is on your steak.

Customer: I can't eat this meat. It's crawling with maggots.
Waiter: Quick! Run to the other end of the table and grab it as it goes.

Customer: Waiter, there's a dead fly in my soup.
Waiter: No, sir, it's a piece of dirt that looks like one.

Customer: Waiter, there's a spider in my soup!
Waiter: Don't worry, sir. There's not enough for it to drown.

Customer: Waiter, what's this cockroach doing on my ice cream sundae?
Waiter: Skiing, sir.

Customer: Why is there a spider in my glass?
Waiter: It scares away the flies.

Customer: Is there soup on the menu?
Waiter: No, sir, I wiped it off.

Customer: This coffee tastes like dirt.
Waiter: That's because it was only ground this morning.

Customer: This bread is stale.
Waiter: That's funny. It wasn't last week.

Customer: What's wrong with these eggs I ordered?
Waiter: Don't ask me, sir. I only laid the table.

A man went into a restaurant and ordered a steak but when the waiter brought it to the table he had his thumb pressed into the meat.

'Are you crazy?' yelled the customer. 'I'm not going to eat that! Why is your thumb on my steak?'

The waiter replied: 'I didn't want it to fall on the floor again.'

A hobo in a greasy spoon diner asked the waitress for a meatloaf dinner and some kind words. She duly brought the meatloaf but didn't say a thing.

'Hey, what about the kind words?' he said.

She whispered: 'Don't eat the meatloaf.'

An American tourist was lunching at a restaurant in Beijing where duck was the speciality of the house. The waiter helpfully explained each dish as he brought it to the table: 'This is breast of duck; this is leg of duck; this is wing of duck.'

Finally came a dish which the American recognized as definitely being chicken. He waited for an explanation but the waiter remained silent. Eventually the American said: 'Well, what's this?'

The waiter replied hesitantly: 'It's friend of duck.'

Working Life

The Devil told a salesman: 'I can make you richer, more famous and more successful than any salesman alive. In fact, I can make you the greatest salesman that ever lived.'

Intrigued, the salesman asked: 'What do I have to do in return?'

The Devil replied: 'You not only have to give me your soul but you also have to give me the souls of your children, the souls of your children's children and indeed the souls of all your descendants throughout eternity.'

'Wait a minute,' said the salesman. 'What's the catch?'

A social worker was walking home late at night when she was confronted by a mugger with a gun.

'Your money or your life!' snarled the mugger.

'I'm sorry,' she replied. 'I'm a social worker. I have no money and no life.'

A man was flying in a hot air balloon when he became aware that he was lost. So he reduced height until he was able to call out to someone on the ground: 'Can you help me? I promised my friend I would meet him half an hour ago but I don't know where I am.'

The man on the ground said: 'You are in a hot air balloon, hovering approximately twenty-five feet above this field. You are between latitude thirty-six and thirty-eight degrees north and between longitude forty and forty-five degrees east.'

'You must be an engineer,' said the balloonist.

'Yes. How did you know?'

'Well,' said the balloonist, 'everything you have told me is technically correct but I have no idea what to make of your information, and the fact is I'm still lost.'

The man on the ground said: 'And you must be a manager.'

'That's right,' said the balloonist. 'How did you know?'

'Because you don't know where you are or where you are going. You have made a promise that you cannot keep and you expect me to solve your problem. The fact is that you are in the same position you were in before we met but now it is somehow my fault.'

A guy was telling a friend about his time working at a large company.

'I tell you, it didn't matter if it was the managing director, the vice presidents or whatever, I always told those guys where to get off.'

'What was your job again?' asked the friend.

'I was the elevator operator.'

A pipe burst in a doctor's house, so he called a plumber. The plumber arrived, unpacked his tools, fiddled around for fifteen minutes, and handed the doctor a bill for three hundred pounds.

The doctor said: 'This is ridiculous! I don't even make that much as a doctor!'

The plumber replied: 'Neither did I when I was a doctor.'

Differences between you and your boss:

When you take a long time, you're slow.
When your boss takes a long time, he's thorough.

When you don't do it, you're lazy.
When your boss doesn't do it, he's too busy.

When you make a mistake, you're an idiot.
When your boss makes a mistake, he's only human.

When you do something without being told, you're overstepping your authority.
When your boss does the same thing, he's using his initiative.

When you stand firm, you're being stubborn.
When your boss takes a stand, he's being firm.

When you're on a day off sick, you're always sick.
When your boss has a day off sick, he must be very ill.

When you apply for leave, you must be going for an interview.
When your boss applies for leave, it's because he's overworked.

A female worker told her boss she was going home early because she didn't feel well. Since the boss was just recovering from illness himself, he wished her well and said he hoped it wasn't something that he'd given her.

'So do I,' she said. 'I've got morning sickness!'

A newly promoted boss decided to stamp his authority on the office by attaching a sign to his door that read: 'I'm the Boss.'

A few days later a colleague took a phone call for him and relayed the message to him in front of the rest of the staff: 'Your wife rang – she wants her sign back.'

Reviewing a potential employee's application form, the manager of a large retail store noted that the candidate had never previously worked in that field.

'I must say that for a man with no experience, you're certainly asking for a high wage.'

'Well,' replied the applicant, 'the work is so much harder when you don't know what you're doing.'

A salesman stopped a man in the street and said: 'Sir, would you like to buy a bottle of this mouthwash for two hundred pounds?'

'Two hundred pounds?' gasped the man. 'You must be joking! That's daylight robbery!'

'Okay,' said the salesman. 'Since you don't seem too happy with that price, I'll sell it to you for one hundred and fifty pounds.'

'You must be crazy,' said the man. 'Nobody's going to pay a hundred and fifty pounds for a bottle of mouthwash. Now get out of my way!'

As the man prepared to go, the salesman grabbed him by the arm and began grovelling. 'Sir, I can see that I've upset you and that really wasn't my intention. By way of apology, let me offer you a chocolate brownie.'

He then took a brownie from his briefcase and handed it to the man.

'Well, okay,' said the man, accepting the brownie, but no sooner had he taken the first bite than he spat it out. 'That's foul!' he yelled. 'It tastes like crap!'

'It is,' said the salesman. 'Wanna buy some mouthwash?'

OUT OF OFFICE REPLIES

You are receiving this automatic notification because I am out of the office. If I was in, chances are you wouldn't have received anything at all.

I am currently out at a job interview and will reply to you if I fail to get the position. Be prepared for my mood.

Sorry to have missed you but I am in hospital having a frontal lobotomy so that I may be promoted to management.

I am on holiday. Your email has been deleted.

Thank you for your message, which has been placed in a queuing system. You are currently in 320th place and can therefore expect to receive a reply sometime in August.

I will be out of the office for the next two weeks for medical reasons. When I return, please refer to me as 'Jenny' instead of 'John'.

A secretary arrived at work late for the third day in a row. The boss summoned her to his office.

'Now look, Sally. I know we had a fling for a while but that's over. I expect you to behave like any other employee. Who told you that you could come and go as you please around here?'

The secretary replied coolly: 'My lawyer.'

A little old lady answered a knock on the door of her remote farmhouse and was confronted by a smartly dressed young man carrying a vacuum cleaner and a bucket.

'Good morning, madam,' he said. 'If I could take a couple of minutes of your time, I would like to demonstrate the very latest in high-powered vacuum cleaners. Believe me, once you have seen how this machine works, you'll never want to go back to your old model.'

'I'm not interested,' she barked. 'I haven't got any money, so clear off!' But as she tried to close the door, he quickly wedged his foot there and kept it open.

'Don't be so hasty,' he said. 'Not until you have at least seen my demonstration.'

And with that he barged past her and emptied a bucket of horse manure over her hallway carpet.

'Madam, if this vacuum cleaner does not remove all traces of this horse manure from your carpet, I will personally eat the remainder.'

'Well, I hope you've got a good appetite,' she said, 'because the electricity was cut off this morning.'

The boss asked a new employee his name. 'Simon,' replied the young man.

The boss scowled. 'I don't know what kind of namby-pamby place you worked at before but we don't use first names here. In my view, it breeds familiarity, which ultimately leads to a breakdown in authority. So I always call employees by their surnames only – Smith, Brown, Jones etc. They in turn refer to me only as Mr Watkins. Understood? Right. Now that we've got that straight, what's your surname?

'Darling,' replied the young man. 'My name is Simon Darling.'

'Okay, Simon, the next thing I want to tell you is ...'.

What employee evaluation comments really mean:

Accepts new job assignments willingly.
Translation: Never finishes anything.

Delegates responsibility effectively.
Translation: Passes the buck.

Alert to company developments.
Translation: The office gossip.

Uses time effectively.
Translation: Clock watcher.

Strong adherence to principles.
Translation: Stubborn.

Average.
Translation: Not too bright.

Competent.
Translation: Able to get work done with help.

Slightly below average.
Translation: Stupid.

Regularly consults with supervisor.
Translation: Pain in the ass.

Gets along with superiors.
Translation: Crawler.

Socially active.
Translation: Drinks heavily.

Straightforward.
Translation: Blunt and insensitive.

Uses all available resources.
Translation: Takes office supplies home for personal use.

Identifies management problems.
Translation: Complains a lot.

Inspires the co-operation of others.
Translation: Gets everyone else to do his work.

Is unusually loyal.
Translation: No other firm wants him.

Meticulous in attention to detail.
Translation: Nitpicker.

Keen sense of humour.
Translation: Tells dirty jokes.

Quick thinking.
Translation: Offers plausible excuses.

Listens well.
Translation: Has no ideas of his own.

Demonstrates qualities of leadership.
Translation: Has a loud voice.

Unblemished character.
Translation: One step ahead of the law.

Should go far.
Translation: Please.

Will go far.
Translation: Boss's relative.

Four men were bragging about how smart their dogs were. The first man was an engineer, the second man was an accountant, the third man was a chemist and the fourth was a government worker.

To show off, the engineer called to his dog: 'T-square, do your stuff.'

T-square trotted over to a desk, took out some paper and a pen and promptly drew a circle, a square and a triangle. Everyone agreed that was pretty smart.

But the accountant said his dog could do better. He called his dog and said: 'Slide Rule, do your stuff.' Slide Rule went out into the kitchen and returned with a dozen cookies. He divided them into four equal piles of three cookies each. Everyone agreed that was good.

But the chemist said his dog could do better. He called his dog and said: 'Measure, do your stuff.' Measure got up, walked over to the fridge, took out a quart of milk, got a ten-ounce glass from the cupboard and poured exactly eight ounces without spilling a drop. Everyone agreed that was impressive.

The three men then turned to the government worker and asked: 'What can your dog do?' The government worker called to his dog and said: 'Coffee Break, do your stuff.' Coffee Break jumped to his feet, ate the cookies, drank the milk, dumped on the circle of paper, assaulted the other three dogs, claimed he injured his back while doing so, filed a grievance report for unsafe working conditions, put in for Worker's Compensation and went home on sick leave.

A boss collared one of his employees strolling in to work at half-past-nine in the morning.

'You should have been here at eight-thirty,' he growled.

'Why?' asked the employee. 'What happened?'

Two builders went into the pub after a hard day's work. They had been drinking for a while when a very smartly dressed man walked in and ordered a drink. The two began to speculate about what the man did for a living.

'I'll bet he's an accountant,' said the first builder.

'Looks more like a stockbroker to me,' argued the second.

They continued to debate the subject for a while until eventually the first builder got another round of drinks in. He saw the smartly dressed man standing at the bar and walked over to him.

'Excuse me, mate, but me and my friend have been arguing over what a smartly dressed fellow like you does for a living.'

Smiling, the man replied: 'I'm a logical scientist.'

'A what?' asked the builder.

'Let me explain,' the man continued. 'Do you have a goldfish at home?'

Puzzled but intrigued, the builder decided to play

along. 'Yes, I do as it happens,' he said.

'Well then, it's logical to assume that you either keep it in a bowl or a pond. Which is it?'

'A pond,' the builder replied.

'Well then, it's logical to assume that you have a large garden.'

The builder nodded his head in agreement.

So the man continued: 'Which means it's logical to assume you have a large house.'

'I have a six bedroom house that I built myself,' the builder said proudly.

'Given that you have such a large house, it's logical to assume that you are married.'

The builder nodded again: 'Yes, I'm married and we have three children.'

'Then it's logical to assume that you have a healthy sex life.'

'Five nights a week!' the builder boasted.

The man smiled: 'Therefore it's logical to assume you don't masturbate often.'

'Never!' the builder exclaimed.

'Well, there you have it,' the man explained, 'that's logical science at work. From finding out that you have a goldfish, I've discovered the size of your garden, all about your house, your family and your sex life!'

The builder left, very impressed by the man's talents. When he returned to his friend, the other builder said: 'I saw you talking to that smart guy. Did you find out what he does?'

'Yeah,' replied the first builder. 'He's a logical scientist.'

'A what?' the second builder asked.

'Let me explain,' the first builder continued. 'Do you have a goldfish at home?'

'No.'

'Well then, you're a tosser!'

An efficiency expert concluded his lecture with the warning: 'Don't try these techniques at home.'

'Why not?' asked a member of the audience.

'Because I watched my wife's routine at breakfast for twenty-five years,' he explained. 'She made up to ten trips between the fridge, the stove, the toaster and the table, almost always carrying a single item at a time. One day I told her: "You're wasting too much time. Why don't you try carrying several things at once?"'

'And did it save time?' asked the man in the audience.

'Yes, it did,' replied the expert. 'It used to take her twenty minutes to make breakfast. Now I do it in ten.'

UNWRITTEN LAWS OF THE OFFICE

A pat on the back is only a few centimetres from a kick in the pants.

You can go anywhere you want if you look serious and carry a clipboard.

The more crap you put up with, the more crap you are going to get.

When the bosses talk about improving productivity, they are never talking about themselves.

There will always be beer cans rolling around the floor of your car when the boss asks for a lift home from the office.

Anyone can do any amount of work provided it isn't the work he is supposed to be doing.

The longer the title, the less important the job.

Machines that have broken down will work perfectly when the repairman arrives.

The last person who quit or was fired will be held responsible for all mistakes.

Important letters that contain no errors will develop errors in the mail.

If it weren't for the last minute, nothing would get done.

Once a job is fouled up, anything done to improve it makes it worse.

The authority of a person is inversely proportional to the number of pens that person is carrying.

You will always get the greatest recognition for the job you least like.

No-one gets sick on Wednesdays.

On his first morning in new premises, a young businessman began sorting out his office. He was in the middle of arranging his desk when there was a knock at the door. Eager to imply that he had gone up in the world and that business was brisk, he quickly picked up the phone and asked the person at the door to come in. A tradesman entered the office but the young businessman talked into the phone as if he were conducting an important conversation with a client.

'I agree,' he said. 'Yes, sure ... Absolutely no problem ... We can do that.'

After a minute, he broke off from his imaginary conversation and said to the tradesman: 'Can I help you?'

'Yes,' replied the tradesman. 'I'm here to hook up the phone.'

Three weeks after a young man had been hired by a top hotel, he was called into the personnel manager's office.

The manager said: 'You told us you had two years' experience at the Dorchester, followed by three years at the Ritz, and that you had organized royal banquets. Now we find that your only previous job was serving in McDonald's!'

'Well,' said the young man. 'In your advert you did say that you wanted someone with imagination!'

An employee went to his boss and said: 'Is there any chance I could have tomorrow off? My wife wants me to help clear out the attic and the garage, and then to fix the guttering.'

'I'm sorry,' said the boss. 'You know we're short-staffed. I can't let you have a day off.'

'Thanks, boss,' said the employee. 'I knew I could count on you!'

The boss of a small firm reluctantly told four of his staff: 'I'm going to have to let one of you go.'

The black employee said: 'I'm a protected minority.'

The female employee said: 'And I'm a woman.'

The oldest employee said: 'Fire me, pal, and I'll hit you with an age discrimination suit so fast it'll make your head spin!'

They all turned to look at the young, white, male employee who thought for a moment before saying: 'I think I might be gay ...'

A shepherd was patiently herding his flock in a remote field when a Jeep Cherokee pulled up in a cloud of dust. Out stepped a young man dripping in designer labels from his Ray-Ban sunglasses to his Gucci shoes.

'Hey, mister,' he called over to the shepherd, 'if I can tell you exactly how many sheep you have in your flock, will you let me have one?'

The shepherd was baffled by this proposition but agreed to go along with it.

So the flash young man stepped out of his Jeep with his laptop under his arm. He hooked himself up to the internet and consulted endless data and spreadsheets, before announcing: 'You have twelve hundred and thirty-eight sheep.'

'That's right,' said the shepherd. 'Fair enough. You can take one of my sheep.'

And he watched while the young man made his selection and loaded it into the Jeep.

'Before you go,' said the shepherd, 'how about letting me have a go? If I can tell you exactly what your job is, will you give me my sheep back?'

'Sure,' said the young man.

'You're a consultant,' said the shepherd

'That's right. How did you know that?'

'Easy,' replied the shepherd. 'You turned up here uninvited. You wanted to be paid for telling me something I already knew. And you don't know anything about my business because you took my dog!'

Experiencing teething troubles with their new computer, a couple phoned the technical help desk. But the guy there insisted on talking to the husband in complex computer jargon, none of which seemed to make much sense.

Eventually, in frustration, the husband said: 'Look, you know what you're talking about but I don't. So can you treat me like a four-year-old and explain it to me that way?'

'Okay, son,' said the technician, 'put your mummy on the phone.'

An employee went to his boss and asked for a day off. 'So you want a day off, do you?' growled the boss. 'Let's take a look at what you asked for.

'There are 365 days this year.

'There are 52 weeks per year in which you already have 2 days off per week, leaving 261 available for work.

'Since you spend 16 hours each day away from work, you have used up 170 days, leaving only 91 available.

'You spend 30 minutes each day on a coffee break. That accounts for 23 days each year, leaving 68 available.

'With an hour for lunch each day, you have used up another 46 days, leaving only 22 days available for work.

'You normally spend 2 days per year on sick leave.

This leaves only 20 days available for work.

'We are off for 5 holidays per year, so your available working time is down to 15 days.

'We generously give you 14 days vacation per year which leaves only 1 day available for work and I'll be damned if you're going to take that day off!'

A boss told his new employee: 'I'll give you ten quid an hour starting today, and in three months I'll raise it to fifteen quid an hour. So when would you like to start?'

The employee replied: 'In three months.'

A young man new to farming bought a thousand baby chicks. A week later, he went back to the supplier and said he needed another thousand baby chicks. Then a week after that, he was back again saying he needed another thousand baby chicks.

'You seem to be having problems,' commented the supplier.

'I don't know what it is,' said the young farmer. 'I'm not sure if I'm planting them too deep or too close together.'

A business consultant died and arrived at the Pearly Gates. To his dismay, there were thousands of people ahead of him in line to see St Peter. So he was surprised when St Peter left his desk at the gate, came down the long line to where the consultant was standing and greeted him warmly. Then St Peter and one of his assistants led the consultant up to the front of the line and sat him in a comfortable chair.

The consultant said: 'I don't mind all this attention but what makes me so special?'

St Peter replied: 'Well, I've added up all the hours for which you billed your clients, and by my calculation you must be about 189 years old!'

A shop steward stood up before the gathering of the workforce to announce the results of protracted negotiations with the employers. 'From next week,' he told his members triumphantly, 'your wages will increase by sixty per cent, you will each get a company house and car, and you will only have to work on Wednesdays.'

'What!' came a cry from the back of the hall. 'Every Wednesday?'

RULES FOR BOSSES

Never give me work in the morning. Always wait until four o'clock and then bring it to me. The challenge of a deadline is always refreshing.

If it's a real rush job, run in and interrupt me every ten minutes to inquire how it's going. That helps. Or even better, hover behind me, advising me at every keystroke.

Always leave without telling anyone where you are going. It gives me a chance to be creative when someone asks where you are.

If my arms are full of papers, boxes or books, don't open the door for me. One day I might need to learn how to function as a paraplegic, so opening doors with no arms is good training.

If you give me more than one job to do, don't tell me which is the most urgent. I am psychic.

If you don't like my work, tell everyone. I like to be talked about.

If I do a job that pleases you, keep it a secret. Otherwise, it could mean promotion.

Do your best to keep me late. I adore this office and really don't have anywhere else to go. I have no life beyond work.

If you have special instructions for a job, don't write them down. Instead save them until the job is almost done. No point in confusing me with useful information.

Never introduce me to the people you are with. I have no right to know anything. In the corporate food chain, I am plankton. When you refer to them later, my shrewd deductions will identify them.

A situations vacant ad called for an experienced lumberjack and at the job interview the applicant was asked to describe his experience.

'I've worked in the Sahara Forest,' he said.

The personnel manager looked puzzled. 'You mean the Sahara Desert?'

'Sure, that's what they call it now!'

A tourist was browsing around a pet shop when a customer came in and said to the shopkeeper: 'Have you got a C monkey?'

The shopkeeper nodded, went over to a large cage at the side of the shop and took out a monkey. Fitting a collar and leash to the monkey, the shopkeeper told the customer: 'That will be five thousand pounds.' The customer paid and left with the monkey.

Startled, the tourist went over to the shopkeeper and said: 'That was a very expensive monkey – most of them are priced at a few hundred pounds. What was so special about it?'

The shopkeeper replied: 'That monkey is invaluable to computer buffs. It can program in C with a very fast, tight code, no bugs. Believe me, it's well worth the money.'

The tourist started to look at the other monkeys in the shop. Pointing at the same cage, he said to the shopkeeper: 'That monkey's even more expensive, ten thousand pounds. What does it do?'

'Oh,' said the shopkeeper, 'that's one's a C++ monkey. It can manage more complex programming, even some Java, all the really useful stuff.'

Then the tourist spotted a third monkey, in a cage of its own. The price tag around its neck said fifty thousand pounds. He asked: 'What on earth does that one do to justify that price?'

The shopkeeper said: 'I don't know if it actually does anything. But it says it's a consultant.'

A civil servant was sitting in his office when out of boredom he decided to see what was in an old filing cabinet. Poking through the dusty contents, he came across an old brass lamp and thought that it would look nice on his mantelpiece at home. So he took it home and while polishing it, a genie suddenly appeared from the lamp and granted him three wishes.

'I wish for an ice cold beer right now,' he began modestly, 'to help me with my next two wishes.'

He received his beer and drank it, then turned his thoughts to his second wish. 'I wish to be on an island inhabited only by beautiful women.'

As if by magic, he found himself on a tropical island surrounded by gorgeous women.

'And what is your third wish?' asked the genie.

The civil servant thought for a second and said: 'I wish I'd never have to work again.'

And POOF! He was back in his office.

'Jeremy is so forgetful,' complained a sales manager to his secretary. 'It's a wonder he can sell anything. He's become a liability. I asked him to pick me up some sandwiches on his way back from lunch but no doubt he'll have forgotten!'

A few minutes later Jeremy bounded in. 'Guess what?' he beamed. 'I was at lunch and who should I bump into but David Austin, an old school friend. It turns out that he's head of a chain of stores that are starting up next month on the south coast, and he's agreed to put a huge order our way. It could be worth a couple of million over the next twelve months. How about that!'

The sales manager turned to his secretary and said: 'See, I told you he'd forget the sandwiches.'

Three boys were standing in the school playground bragging about their fathers.

One said: 'My dad scribbles a few words on a piece of paper, he calls it a poem and they give him five hundred pounds.'

The second said: 'That's nothing. My dad scribbles a few words on a piece of paper, he calls it a song and they give him a thousand pounds.'

The third said: 'I got you both beat. My dad scribbles a few words on a piece of paper, he calls it a sermon and it takes eight people to collect all the money.'

An engineer, a psychologist and a theologian were hunting in the wilderness of Northern Canada. Suddenly the temperature dropped and a fierce snowstorm was upon them. Through the blizzard, they spotted an isolated cabin and, having been told that the locals were hospitable, they knocked on the door in the hope of obtaining respite from the weather. Nobody answered their knocking but when they tried the door, they found that it was unlocked and so they ventured inside.

The cabin was of a basic layout, with nothing out of the ordinary except for the stove. It was large, pot-bellied and made of cast iron but what made it so unusual was its location – it was suspended in mid-air by wires attached to the ceiling beams.

'Fascinating,' said the psychologist. 'It is obvious that this lonely trapper, isolated from humanity, has elevated this stove so that he can curl up under it and vicariously experience a return to the womb.'

'Nonsense!' replied the engineer. 'The man is practising the laws of thermodynamics. By elevating his stove, he has discovered a way to distribute heat more evenly throughout the cabin.'

'With all due respect,' interrupted the theologian, 'I'm sure that hanging his stove from the ceiling has religious significance. Fire lifted up has been a religious symbol for centuries.'

The three debated the point for several hours without resolving the issue. When the cabin owner finally returned, they immediately asked him why he had hung his heavy, pot-bellied stove from the ceiling.

He answered simply: 'Had plenty of wire, not much stove pipe.'

A farmer received a visit from a government official over allegations that he was paying his staff less than the minimum wage. The official asked him for a list of his employees and details of their pay.

'All right,' said the farmer. 'I have a hired man, been with me for three years. I pay him six hundred a week, plus room and board. There's a cook – she's been here six months. She gets five hundred a week, plus room and board.'

'Anybody else?' asked the official as he scribbled on a pad.

'Yeah,' said the farmer. 'There's one guy here is none too bright. He works about eighteen hours a day. I pay him ten pounds a week and a bit of beer money.'

'Aha!' roared the official. 'That's the man I want to talk to!'

'Speaking,' said the farmer.

Jake was fired from his construction job.

'What happened?' asked his friend Joe.

'Well,' explained Jake. 'You know what a foreman is? The one who stands around watching the other men work?'

'Yeah. What of it?'

'Well, he got jealous of me. Everyone thought I was the foreman!'

Three engineers and three accountants were travelling by train. 'I can't get over how expensive my ticket was,' said one of the accountants. 'Fifty pounds for such a short journey.'

'You should do what we do,' advised the chief engineer. 'We three always travel together but only ever buy one ticket. That way, we pay a third of the price each.'

The accountant was mystified. 'But how do you

get away with only buying one ticket? The ticket collector always comes round.'

'It's easy,' said the engineer. 'Watch this.'

At the first sign of the ticket collector, the three engineers huddled into the train toilet and shut the door. When the ticket collector knocked on the door and called 'Ticket please', a single arm held out one ticket. The collector stamped the ticket and went on his way.

The accountant was impressed and, knowing a thing or two about money, decided that he and his two colleagues should try the same trick the next time they travelled together. So the accountants bought just one ticket between them.The engineers happened to be travelling on the same train and, to the accountants' surprise, hadn't even bought one ticket this time.

'You'll never get away with that,' warned the accountants.

'You wait and see,' replied the engineers.

When the ticket collector approached, both groups squeezed together in separate toilets and shut the doors. Then one of the engineers knocked on the door in which the accountants were hiding and said: 'Ticket please.'

While sitting on a park bench, a woman observed two council employees carrying spades and working nearby. She was intrigued to see one man dig a hole and then the other immediately fill it in again. This happened four times until eventually she became so curious that she decided to go over and ask them what they were doing.

Addressing the hole-digger, she said: 'I'm impressed by how hard the two of you are working, but what exactly are you doing? You keep digging a hole and then your partner comes up and fills it in again. I've seen you do this four times in different locations in the park.'

The hole-digger replied: 'I suppose it must look odd but, you see, the guy who plants the trees is off sick today.'

The head of admissions at a school of agriculture asked a prospective student: 'Why have you chosen this particular career?'

The student replied: 'I dream of making a million from farming, like my father.'

The head was impressed. 'Your father made a million from farming?'

'No, but he always dreamed of it.'

Yo Momma ...

AGE

Yo momma's so old, she has hieroglyphics on her driving licence.

Yo momma's so old, she can remember when the Dead Sea was just sick.

Yo momma's so old, her blood type is discontinued.

Yo momma's so old, her breasts squirt out powdered milk.

Yo momma's so old, she was deafened by the Big Bang.

Yo momma's so old, when she was young rainbows were in black and white.

Yo momma's so old, she can't leave fingerprints anymore.

Yo momma's so old, the average age of her friends is deceased.

Yo momma's so old, the candles on her birthday cake raised the Earth's temperature by five degrees.

Yo momma's so old, she's got a signed copy of the Bible.

STUPIDITY

Yo momma's so stupid, she didn't even pass her blood test.

Yo momma's so stupid, her dog teaches her to do tricks.

Yo momma's so stupid, she stood on a chair to raise her IQ.

Yo momma's so stupid, her fingers and toes are numbered.

Yo momma's so stupid, her brain cells die of loneliness.

Yo momma's so stupid, if she was more intelligent she'd be a plant.

Yo momma's so stupid, she was two years old before she got a birthmark.

Yo momma's so stupid, when she went into a think-tank she almost drowned.

Yo momma's so stupid, the only thing she got on her IQ test was drool.

Yo momma's so stupid, she invented a silent car alarm.

Yo momma's so stupid, she invented a new type of parachute that opens on impact.

UGLINESS

Yo momma's so ugly, her lipstick retreats back into the tube.

Yo momma's so ugly, even the tide wouldn't take her out.

Yo momma's so ugly, she practises birth control by leaving the light on.

Yo momma's so ugly, she makes onions cry.

Yo momma's so ugly, her dentist treats her by mail order.

Yo momma's so ugly, people go as her for Halloween.

Yo momma's so ugly, even her shadow won't be seen with her.

Yo momma's so ugly, when she looks in the mirror her reflection ducks.

Yo momma's so ugly, at her wedding everybody kissed the groom.

Yo momma's so ugly, her pillow cries at night.

Yo momma's so ugly, her mother fed her by catapult.

Yo momma's so ugly, even Rice Krispies won't talk to her.

WEIGHT

Yo momma's so fat, the only thing attracted to her is gravity.

Yo momma's so fat, even her shadow has stretch marks.

Yo momma's so fat, she has her own zip code.

Yo momma's so fat, the whole neighbourhood can talk behind her back.

Yo momma's so fat, she shows up on radar.

Yo momma's so fat, she can't play 'hide and seek' – only 'seek'.

Yo momma's so fat, when she cut her leg gravy seeped out.

Yo momma's so fat, she's on both sides of the family.

Yo momma's so fat, she can't even jump to a conclusion.

Yo momma's so fat, her cereal bowl has its own lifeguard.

Yo momma's so fat, her belly button has an echo.

Yo momma's so fat, her plastic surgeon uses scaffolding.

Yo momma's so fat, when she gets in an elevator it has to go down.

Yo momma's so fat, whenever she wears high heels she strikes oil.

Yo momma's so fat, she has stabilizers.